BLACKHALL'S ESSEN… /
REVISION SERIES

Blackhall's Essential Law Revision Series

Constitutional Law

James O'Mahony
Solicitor

Lonsdale Law Publishing

Published by Lonsdale Law Publishing
Lonsdale House
Avoca Avenue
Blackrock
Co. Dublin
Ireland

e-mail: info@lonsdalelawpublishing.com
www.lonsdalelawpublishing.com

Paperback ISBN: 978-1-907325-31-1
ePub ISBN: 978-1-907325-32-8
Kindle ISBN: 978-1-907325-33-5

A catalogue record for this book is available from the British Library.

Printed in Dublin by SPRINT-print Ltd.

Table of Contents

Table of Cases

Table of Statutes

1

Preamble

The Preamble to the Constitution reads as follows:

> 'In the Name of the Most Holy Trinity, from Whom is all authority and to Whom, as our final end, all actions both of men and States must be referred,
>
> We, the people of Éire,
>
> Humbly acknowledging all our obligations to our Divine Lord, Jesus Christ, Who sustained our fathers through centuries of trial,
>
> Gratefully remembering their heroic and unremitting struggle to regain the rightful independence of our Nation,
>
> And seeking to promote the common good, with due observance of Prudence, Justice and Charity, so that the dignity and freedom of the individual may be assured, true social order attained, the unity of our country restored, and concord established with other nations,
>
> Do hereby adopt, enact, and give to ourselves this Constitution.'

Application of the Preamble

Interpretation of Constitutional Provisions

The Preamble has been considered in many decisions in construing the purpose and effect of Constitutional provisions.

- *Attorney General v Southern Industrial Trust*[1]

Lavery J:

> 'The declaration in the preamble, made in general terms, may add little to the more precise terms of the relevant articles. Nevertheless, the words of the preamble declaring the purpose of the people in adopting, enacting, and giving to themselves the Constitution may help in determining the meaning of and the effect to be given to particular provisions.'

- *Buckley v Attorney General*[2]

O' Byrne J:

> 'The [Provisions of the Preamble]...inform the various Articles of the Constitution...[and]...so far as possible, the Constitution should be so construed as to give them life and reality.'

Prudence, Justice and Charity

The reference in the Preamble to the promotion of '*the common good, with due observance of Prudence, Justice and Charity*' has been cited by the judiciary with an acknowledgement that such virtues change over time.

1 (1960) 94 ILTR 161
2 [1950] IR 67

- *McGee v Attorney General*[3]

Walsh J:

> 'It is but natural that from time to time the prevailing ideas of [Prudence, Justice and Charity] may be conditioned by the passage of time; no interpretation of the Constitution is intended to be final for all time. It is given in the light of prevailing ideas and concepts.'

- *The State (Healy) v Donoghue*[4]

O' Higgins CJ:

> '...this preamble makes it clear that rights given by the Constitution must be considered in accordance with concepts of prudence, justice and charity, which may gradually change or develop as society changes and develops and which fall to be interpreted from time to time in accordance with prevailing ideas. The preamble envisages a Constitution which can absorb or be adapted to such changes.'

See also:

- *Attorney General v X*[5]
- *Re Article 26 and the Regulation of Information (Services Out of the State for Termination of Pregnancies Bill) 1995*[6]
- *A v Governor of Arbor Hill Prison*[7]

---

3 [1974] IR 284, (1975) 109 ILTR 29
4 [1976] IR 325, (1976) 110 ILTR 9
5 [1992] 1 IR 1, [1992] ILRM 401,[1992] 2 CMLR 277
6 [1995] 1 IR 1, [1995] 2 ILRM 81
7 [2006] IESC 45

Protection of Rights

The terms of the Preamble referring to the *'dignity and freedom of the individual'* have been identified by the Courts as a basis for the protection of personal rights.

McGee v Attorney General[8]

Henchy J:

> 'The effect of s 17 of the Criminal Law Amendment Act, 1935 [which prohibits the importation of contraceptives] is to condemn the plaintiff and her husband to a way of life which, at best, will be fraught with worry, tension and uncertainty that cannot but adversely affect their lives and, at worst, will result in an unwanted pregnancy causing death or serious illness with the obvious tragic consequences to the lives of her husband and young children. And this in the context of a Constitution which in its preamble proclaims as one of its aims the dignity and freedom of the individual.'

The recognition in the Preamble to the Christian nature of the State was also referred to by Henchy J as evidence that,

> '…the Constitution intended...natural human rights...as being in the category of natural rights derived from God's law.'

[8] [1974] IR 284, (1975) 109 ILTR 29

2

Constitutional Interpretation

Five methods of Constitutional interpretation have been developed by the Irish Courts:

1. Literal Approach
2. Broad Approach
3. Doctrine of Harmonious Interpretation
4. Historical Approach
5. Natural Approach

Literal Approach

Under the literal approach ordinary words are given their ordinary meaning and technical words are given their technical meaning.

- *People (DPP) v O' Shea*[9]

O' Higgins CJ:

> 'The Constitution, as the fundamental law of the State, must be accepted, interpreted and construed according to

[9] [1982] IR 384

> the words which are used; and these words, where the meaning is plain and unambiguous, must be given their literal meaning...Plain words must...be given their plain meaning unless qualified or restricted by the Constitution itself.'

Broad Approach

The broad or purposive approach involves adopting an interpretation which best accords with the objectives of the provision.

- *Attorney General v Paperlink*[10]

Costello J:

> 'The Constitution is a political instrument as well as a legal document and in its interpretation the Courts should not place the same significance on differences of language used in two succeeding sub-paragraphs as would, for example be placed on differently drafted sub-sections of a Finance Act. A purposive, rather than a strictly literal, approach to the interpretation of the sub-paragraphs is appropriate.'

- *O' Sullivan v Robinson*[11]

O' Byrne J:

> 'A Constitution is to be liberally construed so as to carry into effect the intentions of the people embodied therein.'

- *Melling v O'Mathghamhna*[12]

---

10 [1984] ILRM 373

11 [1954] IR 151, (1954) 88 ILTR 169

12 [1962] IR 1, (1962) 97 ILTR 60

O'Dalaigh J:

> '...the Constitution is to be read not as dealing with words but rather with the substance of liberty.'

- *Murray v Ireland*[13]

Costello J determined that the Courts should adopt an approach to interpretation,

> '...which would look at the whole of the text of the Constitution and identify its purpose and objective in protecting human rights.'

- *Quinn Supermarkets v Attorney General*[14]

A provision of the Constitution must be interpreted having regard to the *'spirit and intent'* of that provision.

Harmonious Interpretation

A provision of the Constitution should be construed in accordance with the Constitution in its entirety.This approach to Constitutional interpretation was first recognised by Henchy J in *Dillane v Ireland*[15].

- *State (DPP) v Walsh*[16]

O' Higgins CJ held that a provision of the Constitution should not be interpreted in isolation but

> '...must be construed and considered as part of the Constitution and it should be given a meaning and an application

13 [1985] IR 532, [1985] ILRM 542
14 [1972] IR 1
15 [1980] ILRM 167
16 [1981] IR 412

which does not lead to conflict with other Articles and which conforms with the Constitution's general scheme.'

- *People (DPP) v O' Shea*[17]

Henchy J:

'Any single Constitutional right or power is but a component in an ensemble of interconnected and interacting provisions which must be brought into play as part of a larger composition, and which must be given such an integrated interpretation as will fit harmoniously into the general constitutional order and of modulation. It may be said of such a Constitution, more than of any other legal instrument, that 'the letter killeth, but the spirit giveth life'. No single constitutional provision ...may be isolated and construed with undeviating literalness.'

- *Tormey v Ireland*[18]

Henchy J:

'...the Constitution must be read as a whole and...its several provisions must not be looked at in isolation, but treated as interlocking parts of the general Constitutional scheme.'

Where a harmonious application of Constitutional rights is not possible the Courts, having regard to the doctrine of hierarchy of rights, will examine the hierarchy or priority of conflicting constitutional rights.

- *People v Shaw*[19]

---

17 [1982] IR 384
18 [1985] IR 289, [1985] ILRM 375
19 [1982] IR 1

Kenny J:

> 'There is a hierarchy of Constitutional rights, and, when a conflict arises between them that which ranks higher must prevail...When a conflict of Constitutional rights arises, it must be resolved by having regard to (a) the terms of the Constitution, (b) the ethical values which all Christians living in the State acknowledge and accept, and (c) the main tenets of our system of constitutional parliamentary democracy.'

Historical Approach

The historical approach is the interpretation of the Constitution taking into consideration the state of affairs at the time of enactment of *Bunreacht na hEireann* in order to interpret in accordance with the intentions of those who framed it.

- *Sinnott v Minister for Education*[20]

Murray J:

> 'Agreeing as I do with the view that the Constitution is a living document which falls to be interpreted in accordance with contemporary circumstances including prevailing ideas and mores, this does not mean, and I do not think it has ever been so suggested, that it can be divorced from its historical context. Indeed, by definition that which is contemporary is determined by reference to its historical context.'

- *McGee v Attorney General*[21]

---

[20] [2001] 2 IR 545

[21] [1974] IR 284, (1975) 109 ILTR 29

Walsh J:

> '...it is but natural that from time to time the prevailing ideas of prudence, justice and charity may be conditioned by the passage of time; no interpretation of the Constitution is intended to be final for all time.'

- *State (Healy) v Donoghue*[22]

O' Higgins CJ:

> '...rights given by the Constitution must be considered in accordance with the concepts of prudence, justice and charity which may gradually change or develop as society changes and develops and which fall to be interpreted from time to time in accordance with prevailing ideas.'

- *Norris v Attorney General*[23]

McCarthy J:

> '...it would be plainly impossible to identify with the necessary degree of accuracy of description the standards or mores of the Irish People of 1937 - indeed, it is no easy task to so today...In my view, it passes from the reality of legal fiction into the world of unreality if the test sought to be applied is one based on some question such as 'Did the people of Saorstát Éireann in 1937 consider that the offence created by some Victorian Statute should no longer be in force?'

- *Zappone and Gilligan v Revenue Commissioners*[24]

---

22 [1976] IR 325, (1976) 110 ILTR 9
23 [1984] IR 36
24 [2006] IEHC 404

Dunne J:

> 'Marriage was understood under the 1937 Constitution to be confined to persons of the opposite sex...there is a difference between an examination of the Constitution in the context of ascertaining unenumerated rights and redefining a right which is implicit in the Constitution and which is clearly understood. In this case the Court is being asked to redefine marriage to mean something which it has never done to date...The definition of marriage to date has always been understood as being opposite sex marriage...I do not see how marriage can be redefined by the Court to encompass same sex marriage.'

Natural Approach

The natural law approach involves devising an interpretation based on the law of God or a system of beliefs or ethics considered to be inherent in human nature.The natural law approach is particularly applied to reach a construction which accords with the Christian and democratic nature of the State.

Ryan v Attorney General[25]

Kenny J:

> 'Natural law is both anterior and superior to man-made law. There are many personal rights of citizens which flow from the Christian and democratic nature of the State which are not mentioned in Article 40 at all.'

[25] [1965] IR 294

The natural law approach to constitutional interpretation was rejected in *TD v Minister for Education*[26] and *Re Article 26* and the *Regulation of Information (Service out of the State for Termination of Pregnancies) Bill 1995*[27].

26 [2001] 4 IR 259 (Supreme Court), 2000 2 ILRM 321 (High Court)
27 [1995] 1 IR 1, [1995] 2 ILRM 81

3

Royal Prerogatives

Royal prerogatives consist of certain powers, privileges and immunities vested in the Crown. The Irish State assumed such royal prerogatives as successor to the Crown. However, in *Byrne v Ireland*[28] and *Webb v Ireland*[29] it was determined that the royal prerogatives did not survive the creation of the Irish Free State.

Byrne v Ireland

Walsh J:

> 'The State is the creation of the People and is to be governed in accordance with the provisions of the Constitution which was enacted by the people and which can be amended by the people only... the governing authority is the people... All royal prerogatives to be found in the common law of England and in the common law of Ireland prior to the enactment of the Constitution of Saorstát Éireann, *1922*, ceased to be part of the law of Saorstát Éireann because they were based on concepts expressly repudiated by Article 2 of that Constitution and, therefore,

[28] [1972] IR 241

[29] [1988] IR 353, [1988] ILRM 565

> were inconsistent with the provisions of that Constitution and were not carried over by Article 73.'

Webb v Ireland

Finlay CJ cited with approval the decision in Byrne and affirmed that:

> '...no royal prerogative in existence prior to the enactment of the Constitution of 1922 was by virtue of the provisions of that Constitution vested in the Irish Free State.'

The Courts have determined that the following royal prerogatives no longer exist:

- immunity from suit: *Byrne v Ireland*[30]
- treasure trove: *Webb v Ireland*[31]
- exemption from application of statutes: *Howard v Commissioners of Public Works*[32]
- priority of Crown debts on the administration of an insolvent estate: *Re PC: an Arranging Debtor*[33], *Re Irish Employers Mutual Insurance Association Ltd*[34].

30 [1972] IR 241
31 [1988] IR 353, [1988] ILRM 565
32 [1993] ILRM 665
33 [1939] IR 306, (1939) 73 ILTR 84
34 [1955] IR 176

4

Separation of Powers

The three branches of Government are the *legislature*, the *executive* and the *judiciary*. The Constitution confers specific functions on each of these arms of Government and, under the doctrine of separation of powers, no branch of government can perform functions vested in another.

Legislative Function

Article 15.2

> '1° The sole and exclusive power of making laws for the State is hereby vested in the Oireachtas: no other legislative authority has power to make laws for the State.
>
> 2° Provision may however be made by law for the creation or recognition of subordinate legislatures and for the powers and functions of these legislatures.'

Therefore, pursuant to Article 15.2.1, the power to make law is vested in the Oireachtas. However, Article 15.2.2 permits the delegation of legislation function to subordinate legislatures where provision is made for this in the parent act.

Delegated legislation must comply with the principles and policies test established by O' Higgins CJ in *City View Press v AnCo*[35]:

> '…the test is whether that which is challenged as an unauthorised delegation of parliamentary power is more than a mere giving effect to principles and policies which are contained in the statute itself. If it be, then it is not authorised; for such would constitute a purported exercise of legislative power by an authority which is not permitted to do so under the Constitution. On the other hand, if it be within the permitted limits - if the law is laid down in the statute and details only are filled in or completed by the designated Minister or subordinate body - there is no unauthorised delegation of legislative power.'

The delegation of legislative function will be unconstitutional where the parent act does not contain principles or policies. The delegated legislation will be ultra vires where it exceeds the principles and policies contained in the parent act.

Note also:

- *Harvey v Minister for Social Welfare*[36],
- *Cook v Walsh*[37],
- *McDaid v Sheehy*[38],
- *Mulcreevy v Minister for Environment*[39],

---

35 [1980] IR 381
36 [1990] 2 IR 232
37 [1984] IR 710
38 [1991] I IR 1
39 [2004] 1 ILRM 419

- *DPP v Leontjava*[40],
- *In re Article 26 and the Health (Amendment)(No. 2) Bill 2004*[41],
- *Laurentiu v Minister for Justice*[42],
- *Bupa Ireland v Health Insurance Authority*[43]

It should be noted however that Article 15 does not apply to ministerial administrative arrangements or direction [*Casey v Minister for Arts, Heritage, Gaeltacht and the Islands*[44], *Dunne v Minister for Arts, Heritage, Gaeltacht and the Islands*[45]].

National Legislation Introducing European Union Law

In relation to the implementation of the provisions of European Union law a ministerial regulation may be appropriate where the principles and policies to be applied are stipulated in the corresponding European measure.

Where the principles and policies are not so stipulated and national authorities have discretion to determine the principles and policies to be applied then legislation is required.

More specifically in *Meagher v Minister for Agriculture*[46] Denham J held that:

40 [2004] 1 IR 591
41 [2005] 1 IR 105
42 [1999] 4 IR 26, [2000] 1 ILRM 1
43 [2006] IEHC 431
44 [2004] IESC 14
45 [2006] IESC 49, [2007] 1 ILRM 264, [2007] 1 IR 194
46 [1994] 1 IR 329, [1994] 1 ILRM 1

> 'If the directive left to the national authority matters of principle or policy to be determined then the 'choice' of the Minister would require legislation by the Oireachtas. But where there is no case made that principles or policies have to be determined by the national authority, where the situation is that the principles and policies were determined in the directive, then legislation by a delegated form, by regulation, in a valid choice. The fact that an Act of the Oireachtas has been affected by the policy in a directive, is a 'result to be achieved' wherein there is now no choice between the policy and the national Act. The policy of the directive must succeed. Thus where there is in fact no choice on a policy or a principle it is a matter appropriate for delegated legislation. If the directive or the Minister envisaged any choice of principle or policy then it would require legislation by the Oireachtas.'

Note also: *Maher v Minister for Agriculture*[47].

Judicial Interference with Legislation Function

The Courts must apply the law as created by the legislature.

It is a breach of the doctrine of separation of powers for the judiciary to create law or apply law contrary to statutory provision.

De Gortari v Smithwick (No. 2)[48]

McGuinness J:

> '...[a judge cannot] legislate to fill in gaps left by the legislature.'

---

47 [2001] 2 IR 139, [2001] 2 ILRM 481
48 [2000] IEHC 5, [2001] 1 ILRM 354, [2000] 2 IR 553

McGrath v McDermott[49]

Finlay CJ:

> '...[it is not permissible to] add to or delete from express statutory provision so as to achieve objectives which to the courts appear desirable.'

Judicial Function

Administration of Justice

Article 34.1 of the Constitution provides that:

> 'Justice shall be administered in Courts established by law by judges appointed in the manner provided by this Constitution, and, save in such special and limited cases as may be prescribed by law, shall be administered in public.'

Therefore,the function of the judiciary is to administer justice. There will be a breach of Article 34.1 and the separation of powers doctrine where justice is administered by a body other than the Courts.

The characteristics of an administration of justice were outlined by Kenny J in *McDonald v Bord Na gCon (No. 2)*[50]:

> '1. A dispute or controversy as to the existence of legal rights or a violation of the law.
>
> 2. The determination or ascertainment of the rights of parties or the imposition of liabilities or the infliction of a penalty.
>
> 3. The final determination (subject to appeal) of legal rights, liabilities or the imposition of penalties.

[49] [1988] IR 258, [1988] ILRM 647

[50] [1965] IR 217

4. The enforcement of those rights or liabilities or the imposition of a penalty by the Court or by the executive power of the State which is called in by the Court to enforce its judgment.
5. The making of an order by the Court which as a matter of history is an order being characteristic of Courts in this Country.'

where proceedings have characteristics 1–5 any such matter can only be determined by the court. In addition criminal proceedings must be heard in the courts.

In *Re Haughey*[51] O'Dalaigh CJ held that:

> '...the Constitution vests the judicial power of Government solely in the Courts and reserve exclusively to the Courts the power to try a person on criminal charges. Trial, conviction and sentence are indivisible parts of the exercise of this power.'

Performance of Limited Judicial Functions

Article 37.1:

> '...nothing in this Constitution shall operate to invalidate the exercise of limited functions and powers of a judicial nature in matters other than criminal matters by any person or body of persons duly authorised by law to exercise such functions and powers, notwithstanding that such person or such body of persons is not a judge or a Court appointed or established under this Constitution.'

Whether the exercise of functions or powers of a judicial nature are 'limited' will depend on the impact of such functions or powers on the individual.

---

[51] [1971] IR 217

Melton Enterprises v Censorship of Publications Board[52]
Keane CJ:

'If the exercise of the assigned powers and functions is calculated ordinarily to affect in the most profound and far reaching way the lives, liberties, fortunes or reputations of those against whom they are exercised they cannot possibly be described as 'limited'.'

Re Solicitors Act 1954[53]
Kingsmill Moore J:

'A tribunal having a few powers and functions but those of far reaching effect and importance [such as the loss of profession] could not properly be regarded as exercising limited powers and functions ... The test as to whether a power is or is not 'limited' in the opinion of the court, lies in the effect of the assigned power when exercised. If the exercise of the assigned powers and functions is calculated ordinarily to affect in the most profound and far reaching way the lives, liberties, fortunes or reputations of those against whom they are exercised they cannot possibly be described as 'limited'.'

See also:
M v Medical Council[54]
By contrast, O' Flaherty J in *Keady v The Commissioner of An Garda Síochána*[55] found that:

'Membership of [An Garda Síochána] carries rights and privileges not possessed by other citizens; it also involves onerous duties not shared by others. The force could not

52 [2003] 3 IR 623
53 [1960] IR 239
54 [1984] IR 485
55 [1992] ILRM 312

properly carry out its essential function of preserving law and order unless there was an entitlement in the commissioner to enforce discipline which necessarily involves the ultimate sanction of dismissal from the force for sufficiently grave breaches of discipline........while a Garda who is dismissed loses his immediate employment he does not lose any qualification by virtue of his dismissal...'

In *Maguire v Ardagh*[56] (the Abbeylara decision) the Supreme Court determined that Oireachtas committees could not undertake an investigation/inquiry into the conduct of an individual who was not a member of the Oireachtas.

Hardiman J found that:

'I cannot see that either as a private citizen or as a member of An Garda Síochána any of the applicants are directly and individually accountable to the Oireachtas at common law or by statute...If any citizen, garda or otherwise, is to be directly accountable in general or in some circumstances, to the Oireachtas, I believe such accountability must be imposed by statute...If the Oireachtas were enabled to send for any citizen and to reach findings of fact or conclusions which could be adverse to him and affect his reputation and his employment, it would indeed be functioning as a 'High Court of Parliament'...I have not heard anything that convinces me that there is in our Constitution anything which confers such a power on the Oireachtas, either in relation to civil or public servants or in relation to citizens generally.'

The proceedings of a tribunal of inquiry do not constitute an administration of justice.

[56] [2002] 1 IR 385

In *Murphy & Ors v Mr. Justice Flood & Ors*[57] Hardiman J cited with approval the decision of Costello J in *Goodman International v Mr. Justice Hamilton*[58]:

> 'In the words of Costello J, or in the words of the judicial authorities cited with approval by him, the Tribunal of Inquiry is 'not imposing any liabilities or affecting any rights'...its conclusions have merely the status of opinion and 'this opinion is devoid of legal consequences'..., its findings are 'sterile of legal effect'...and its purpose is 'merely' to inquire and report...A Tribunal of Inquiry is 'a simple fact-finding-operation'...The Tribunal has no power to inflict a penalty and its determinations cannot 'form any basis for the punishment by any other authority of that person'... Its function is to 'make a finding of fact, in effect, in vacuo, and to report it to the Legislature'...'

Note also:

Haughey v Moriarty[59],
Director of Corporate Enforcement v Bailey[60].

Executive Function

Article 28.2

> 'The executive power of the State shall, subject to the provisions of this Constitution, be exercised by or on the authority of the Government.'

---

57 [2000] 2 IR 298
58 [1992] ILRM 145
59 [1999] 3 IR 1
60 [2011] IESC 24

Article 29.4.1

> 'The executive power of the State in or in connection with its external relations shall in accordance with Article 28 of this Constitution be exercised by or on the authority of the Government.'

Executive function consists of the residual powers of Government excepting legislative and judicial functions.

Boland v An Taoiseach[61]

Fitzgerald CJ:

> 'Consequently, in my opinion, the Courts have no power, either express or implied, to supervise or interfere with the exercise by the Government of its executive functions, unless the circumstances are such as to amount to a clear disregard by the Government of the powers and duties conferred upon it by the Constitution.'

The Courts and Non-Justiciable Controversies

In *Tormey v Ireland*[62] Henchy J advised that the Courts have jurisdiction to consider 'all justiciable matters and questions.'

The Courts do not have competence to consider non-justiciable matters which are exclusively within the jurisdiction of the executive or Oireachtas.

The Ccourts therefore cannot determine, *inter alia*, matters of external relations, foreign affairs and national defence [*Macken v An Taoiseach*[63], *Boland v An Taoiseach*[64]].

61 [1974] IR 338, (1975) 109 ILTR 13
62 [1985] IR 289, [1985] ILRM 375
63 (1984) Irish Times, 26 May
64 [1974] IR 338, (1975) 109 ILTR 13

The Courts cannot interfere with the legislative process, Constitutional amendments or the conduct of referenda [*Finn v Attorney General*[65], *Roche v Ireland*[66], *Slattery v An Taoiseach*[67], *Riordan v An Taoiseach*[68]].

However in *McKenna v An Taoiseach (No. 2)*[69] Hamilton CJ determined that:

> '1. The Courts have no power, either express or implied, to supervise or interfere with the exercise by the Government of its executive functions provided that it acts within the restraints imposed by the Constitution on the exercise of such powers.
>
> 2. If, however, the Government acts otherwise than in accordance with the provisions of the Constitution and in clear disregard thereof, the Courts are not only entitled but obliged to intervene.
>
> 3. The Courts are only entitled to intervene if the circumstances are such as to amount to a clear disregard by the Government of the powers and duties conferred on it by the Constitution.'

The Courts cannot direct the executive on the distribution or allocation of resources.

In *State (C) v Frawley*[70] Finlay P acknowledged that:

> '...it is not the function of the Court to recommend to the executive what is desirable or to fix the priorities of its health and welfare policy.'

---

65 [1983] IR 154
66 17 June 1983, unreported, High Court
67 1993 1 IR 286
68 [2000] 4 IR 537
69 [1995] 2 IR 10, [1996] 1 ILRM 81
70 [1976] IR 365

In *O' Reilly v Limerick Corporation*[71] Costello J held that any claim relating to the unjust distribution on national wealth (distributive justice) should "...be advanced in Leinster House rather than in the Four Courts" and in *TD v Minister for Justice*[72] Keane CJ determined that:

> '...the granting of an order [requiring the executive power of the State to be implemented in a specific manner by the expenditure of money on defined objects within particular time limits] is inconsistent with the distribution of powers between the legislative, executive and judicial arms of Government mandated by the Constitution.'

In *Sinnott v Minister for Education*[73] Keane CJ held that

> '...this Court would not grant mandatory relief requiring the Oireachtas to provide funds for a particular purpose in order to uphold the constitutional or purely legal rights of members of the public.'

The Courts may interfere where Constitutional rights are being undermined by the performance of or the failure to perform executive function: *FN v Minister for Education*[74], *DB v Minister for Justice*[75], *McMenamin v Ireland*[76], *TD v Minister for Justice*[77].

---

71 [1989] ILRM 181
72 [2001] 4 IR 259 (Supreme Court), 2000 2 ILRM 321 (High Court)
73 [2001] 2 IR 545
74 [1995] 1 IR 409
75 [1999] 1 ILRM 93
76 [1996] 3 IR 100
77 [2001] 4 IR 259 (Supreme Court), 2000 2 ILRM 321 (High Court)

5

The Oireachtas

The Oireachtas consists of the Dáil and the Seanad. Article 15 of the Constitution sets out certain procedural aspects of the Houses of the Oireachtas. Articles 16 and 17 relate to Dáil Éireann. Article 16 deals with issues such as eligibility for Dáil membership, the voting rights of citizens in Dáil elections, the conduct of general elections and the Constitutional requirements concerning constituencies for Dáil Éireann. Article 17 (together with Articles 21 and 22) sets out the financial function of Dáil Éireann. Articles 18 and 19 relate to the Seanad and, in particular, set out the composition of the Seanad and the rules for electing members to the Seanad. The legislative process is outlined in Article 23 and Articles 21-22 outline the procedure for the initiation of money bills.

Dail Constituencies

Article 16.2 of the Constitution provides that:

> '1. Dáil Éireann shall be composed of members who represent constituencies determined by law.

2. The number of members shall from time to time be fixed by law, but the total number of members of Dáil Éireann shall not be fixed at less than one member for each thirty thousand of the population, or at more than one member for each twenty thousand of the population.
3. The ratio between the number of members to be elected at any time for each constituency and the population of each constituency, as ascertained at the last preceding census, shall, so far as it is practicable, be the same throughout the country.
4. The Oireachtas shall revise the constituencies at least once in every twelve years, with due regard to changes in distribution of the population, but any alterations in the constituencies shall not take effect during the life of Dáil Éireann sitting when such revision is made.'

O' Donovan v Attorney General[78]

Budd J:

'... the dominant principle of [Article 16.2.3] is the achievement as near an equality of the parliamentary representation of the population as can be attained, paying due regard to practical difficulties.'

Budd J concluded however that:

'Parity of ratio...is to be attained as far as that is capable of being carried into action in a practical way, having regard to such practical difficulties as exist and may legitimately be taken into consideration. That does not involve taking mere matters of convenience into consideration... [Such difficulties are of an administrative and statistical nature so plain to be seen that it may be safely assumed they, at

78 [1961] IR 114, (1962) 96 ILTR 121

any rate, must have been in the minds of those enacting the Constitution.'

Article 26 and the Electoral (Amendment) Bill 1961[79]

Maguire CJ:

'... exact parity in the ratio between members and the population of each constituency is unlikely to be obtained and is not required. The decision as to what is practical is within the jurisdiction of the Oireachtas. It may reasonably take into consideration a variety of factors, such as the desirability so far as possible to adhere to well known boundaries such as those of counties, townlands and electoral divisions. The existence of divisions created by such physical features as rivers, lakes and mountains may also have to be reckoned with.'

Maguire CJ held however that, while the problem of what is practical is primarily one for the Oireachtas, the Courts can pronounce whether the ratio of Dail members to constituency population is a violation of Article 16.2.3.

O' Malley v An Taoiseach[80]

Hamilton P:

'... the Oireachtas is obliged to revise the constituencies with due regard to changes in distribution of the population' particularly 'when a census return discloses major changes.'

Murphy & Anor v Minister for the Environment & Ors[81]

[79] [1961] 1 IR 169
[80] [1990] ILRM 461
[81] [2007] IEHC 185 (2007)

Clarke J:

> '....the immediate consequence of the publication of census figures which show that the constituencies then currently provided for by law are no longer proportional 'so far as it is practicable', leads to a situation where the Oireachtas has an immediate and pressing obligation to put in place measures designed to remedy that problem by enacting appropriate amending legislation.'

In *Doherty v Government of Ireland*[82] the High Court found that the Constitutional right of the citizen to representation in Dáil Éireann required that a by-election should be held within a reasonable timeframe of a vacancy arising. Kearns J held that:

> 'It seems to me that a citizen's constitutional rights are trenched upon and significantly diluted when no effect is given to rights for representation clearly delineated in the Constitution. These are rights which might usefully be characterised as forming part of the "Constitutional contract" between the citizen and the State.'

Membership of the Dáil and Right to Stand for Election

Article 16.1.1:

> 'Every citizen without distinction of sex who has reached the age of twenty-one years, and who is not placed under disability or incapacity by this Constitution or by law, shall be eligible for membership of Dáil Éireann.'

King v Minister for the Environment[83]

82 [2010] IEHC 369
83 [2004] 3 IR 345

In this case, Kearns J held that the Oireachtas may legislate to restrict candidature for Dáil elections "when it has good policy reasons for doing so" and any such restriction is proportionate.

Kelly v Minister for Environment[84]

McKechnie J:

> '…the principle of equality must apply to all candidates seeking election or re-election, as the case may be. This does not however necessarily mean that uniformity must follow in all circumstances. Where however there is a difference, such a difference must be legitimately based and must be justified on both objective and reasonable grounds. In addition in respect of all such candidates, the concept of fairness and basic fair procedures likewise apply.'

Right to Vote

Article 16.1.2:

'(i) All citizens, and

(ii) such other persons in the State as may be determined by law, without distinction of sex who have reached the age of eighteen years who are not disqualified by law and comply with the provisions of the law relating to the election of members of Dáil Éireann, shall have the right to vote at an election for members of Dáil Éireann.'

Accordingly all citizens who have reached the age of eighteen have the right to vote.

[84] [2002] 4 IR 191

However in *Breathnach v Ireland*[85] the Supreme Court recognised that the right to vote was not absolute and cited with approval the decision of O'Higgins CJ in *Draper v Attorney General*[86] that:

> 'In the opinion of the Court the present law, contained in the Electoral Act, provides a reasonable regulation of elections to *Dáil Éireann*, having regard to the obligation of secrecy, the need to prevent abuses and other requirements of the common good. The fact that some voters are unable to comply with its provisions does not of itself oblige the State to tailor that law to suit their special needs. The State may well regard the cost and risk involved in providing special facilities for particular groups as not justified, having regard to the numbers involved, their wide dispersal throughout the country and the risks of electoral abuses.'

Oireachtas Rules and Standing Orders

Article 15.10

> 'Each House shall make its own rules and standing orders, with power to attach penalties for their infringement, and shall have power to ensure freedom of debate, to protect its official documents and the private papers of its members, and to protect itself and its members against any person or persons interfering with, molesting or attempting to corrupt its members in the exercise of their duties.'

The courts do not intrude upon the internal workings of the Oireachtas: *O' Malley v Ceann Comhairle*[87].

---

85 [2000] IEHC 53

86 [1984] IR 277

87 [1997] 1 IR 427

Maguire v Ardagh[88]

> 'Different considerations apply however, where... the Oireachtas purports to establish a committee empowered to enquire and make findings on matters which may unarguably affect the good name and reputations of citizens who are not members of either House.'

Cabinet Confidentiality

Cabinet confidentiality refers to the right of government to withhold documentation relating to cabinet meetings and discussions.

However, in *Murphy v Dublin Corporation*[89] the Supreme Court determined that the executive could not prevent the judiciary from examining documentation pertaining to Government meetings which were relevant to an issue at trial in order to determine whether any such document should be produced. Walsh J:

> 'Having regard to the nature of the powers of the Courts in these matters, it seems clear to me that there can be no documents which may be withheld from production simply because they belong to a particular class of documents. Each document must be decided upon having regard to the considerations which apply to that particular document and its contents. To grant or withhold the production of a document simply by reason of the class to which it belongs would be to regard all documents as being of equal importance notwithstanding that they may not be. In my view, once the court is satisfied that the document is relevant, the burden of satisfying the Court

88 [2002] 1 IR 385
89 [1972] IR 215, (1973) 107 ILTR 65

that a particular document ought not to be produced lies upon the party, or the person, who makes such a claim.'

The decision in *Murphy* was affirmed by the Supreme Court in *Ambiorix Ltd v Minister for the Environment*[90] wherein McCarthy J espoused that:

> 'The Constitution guarantees fair procedures in the administration of justice; discovery of documents is part of those procedures........ I reject the challenge made to the decision in Murphy; in particular I reject the claim that documents may be withheld from production simply because they belong to a particular class.'

However the confidentiality of meetings of Government was firmly asserted by the Supreme Court in *Attorney General v Hamilton*[91]. Hederman J held that cabinet confidentiality was premised on the collective unity of government referred to in Article 28.4.2 which provides that:

> 'The Government shall meet and act as a collective authority, and shall be collectively responsible for the Departments of State administered by the members of the Government.'

Hederman J found that:

> 'It is very clear from the very nature of collective responsibility of the Government that discussions among its members at their formal meetings must be confidential otherwise its decisions are liable to be fatally weakened by disclosure of dissenting views....'

---

90 [1992] 1 IR 277
91 [1993] 2 IR 250

Article 28.4.3, of the Constitution, expressly provides for the confidentiality of government meetings subject to judicial control:

> 'The confidentiality of discussions at meetings of the Government shall be respected in all circumstances save only where the High Court determines that disclosure should be made in respect of a particular matter -
>
> (i) in the interests of the administration of justice by a Court, or
>
> (ii) by virtue of an overriding public interest, pursuant to an application in that behalf of a tribunal appointed by the Government or a Minister of the Government on the authority of the Houses of the Oireachtas to inquire into a matter stated by them to be of public importance.'

Oireachtas Privilege

The privilege of Oireachtas members is contained in Articles 15.12 and 15.13 of the Constitution:

> '12. All official reports and publications of the Oireachtas or of either House thereof and utterances made in either House wherever published shall be privileged.
>
> 13. The members of each House of the Oireachtas shall, except in case of treason as defined in this Constitution, felony or breach of the peace, be privileged from arrest in going to and returning from, and while within the precincts of, either House, and shall not, in respect of any utterance in either House, be amenable to any court or any authority other than the House itself.'

- *Attorney General v Hamilton (No. 2)*[92]

A statement uttered in either House of the Oireachtas is privileged and, accordingly, a Dáil deputy or member of the Seanad cannot be the subject of civil or criminal proceedings as a result of any such statement.

However, "[A] voluntary conscious deliberate repetition" outside the Oireachtas of utterances made in the Dáil or Seanad is not privileged.

- *Garda Representative Authority v Ireland*[93]

Statements made in either House can be relied upon as evidence in proceedings which do not pertain to issues of civil and criminal liability of the Dáil or Seanad member.

92 [1993] 3 IR 227
93 [1989] IR 193

6

Courts and Judiciary

Courts

Article 34 of the Constitution sets out the Constitutional foundation of the Court system in Ireland.

Article 34.1 provides that justice shall be administered in the Courts and Article 34.2 states that the Courts shall consist of Courts of first instance and a Court of final appeal.

Supreme Court: Article 34.4

- The Court of Final Appeal shall be called the Supreme Court.
- The Supreme Court has, with such exceptions and subject to such regulations as may be prescribed by law, appellate jurisdiction from all decisions of the High Court, and shall also have appellate jurisdiction from such decisions of other Courts as may be prescribed by law.
- The decision of the Supreme Court is final and conclusive in all cases.

High Court: Article 34.3

- The High Court is vested with full original jurisdiction in and power to determine all matters and questions whether of law or fact, civil or criminal.
- The High Court has jurisdiction to consider the question of the validity of any law having regard to the provisions of the Constitution.

District Court and Circuit Court: Article 34.3.4

The Courts of First Instance include Courts of local and limited jurisdiction with a right of appeal as determined by law.

Special Criminal Court: Article 38.3

Special Courts may be established by law for the trial of offences where it is determined that the ordinary Courts are inadequate to secure the effective administration of justice, and the preservation of public peace and order.

Administration of Justice in Public

Article 34.1 states that justice shall be administered in public save in such special and limited cases as may be prescribed by law.

Re R Limited[94]
Walsh J:

[94] [1989] IR 126

'...[the administration of justice in public is] a fundamental principle of the administration of justice in a democratic state'[and] does require that the doors of the Courts must be open so that members of the general public may come and see for themselves that justice is done.'

Note also: *Irish Press Plc v Ingersoll Irish Publications Ltd*[95]

The stipulation that justice must be administered in public necessitates identifying the parties to the proceedings: *Roe v Blood Transfusion Board Service Board*[96], *Re Ansbacher (Cayman) Ltd*[97], *Doe v Revenue Commissioners*[98].

Re Ansbacher (Cayman) Ltd[99]
McCracken J:

'...the right to have justice administered in public far exceeds any right to privacy, confidentiality or a good name.'

However, in relation to media reporting of criminal proceedings, Hamilton CJ in *Irish Times v Ireland*[100] held:

'...a trial judge was under an obligation to hold the trial in public and not to interfere or in any way restrict the right of the media to publish a fair and accurate report of the proceedings publicly heard before the Court unless such publication is prohibited by law or would interfere with or prejudice an accused person's right to a fair trial.'

---

95 [1994] 1 IR 176, [1993] ILRM 747
96 [1996] 3 IR 67
97 [2002] 2 IR 517, [2002] ILRM 491
98 [2008] 3 IR 328
99 [2002] 2 IR 517, [2002] ILRM 491
100 [1998] 1 IR 359, [1998] 2 ILRM 161

Classification of Offences

Minor/Summary Offences: Article 38.2

> 'Minor offences may be tried by courts of summary jurisdiction.'

Re Haughey[101]

O'Dalaigh CJ:

> 'A Court of summary jurisdiction within the meaning of [Article 38.2] is one whose criminal jurisdiction to try and to convict is restricted to the trial of minor offences.... Under our law that jurisdiction is exercised only by the District Court.'

A minor offence is one which is tried by judge only in the District Court. A major or indictable offence is tried by judge and jury.

Factors determining the nature of an offence

- The severity of the punishment: *Melling v O' Mathghamhna*[102], *Conroy v Attorney General*[103], *Re Haughey*.[104]
- Regard should be given to:
  - the statutory penalty and not that actually imposed on an accused: *Re Haughey*[105],
  - the primary punishment and not secondary consequences (such as disqualification from driving

[101] [1971] IR 217
[102] [1962] IR 1, (1963) 97 ILTR 60
[103] [1965] IR 411
[104] [1971] IR 217
[105] [1971] IR 217

or revocation of a licence): *Conroy v Attorney General*[106],

- ◦ the potential loss to an accused by forfeiture of property if convicted: *L'Henryenat v Ireland*[107], *O'Sullivan v Hartnett and the Attorney General*[108],

- The moral nature of the act: *Melling v O'Mathghamhna*[109], *Conroy v Attorney General*[110].

A minor offence is considered to be one which involves the imposition of a maximum fine of €3,000 and/or a maximum term of imprisonment of 1 year.

Trial by Jury:

Article 38.5

> 'Save in the case of the trial of offences under section 2, section 3 or section 4 of this Article no person shall be tried on any criminal charge without a jury.'

De Burca & Anderson v Attorney General[111]
Griffin J:

> 'The purpose of a jury is to interpose between the State and the accused person an impartial body of the accused's fellow citizens to try the issue joined between the prosecution and the accused. Therefore, in my opinion, the jury should be a body which is truly representative, and a fair cross-section, of the community.'

---

106 [1965] IR 411
107 [1983] IR 193, [1984] ILRM 249
108 [1983] ILRM 79
109 [1962] IR 1, (1963) 97 ILTR 60
110 [1965] IR 411
111 [1976] IR 38

The trial judge determines issues of law and the jury decides issues of fact.

The distinct roles of the judge and jury were outlined by Henchy J in *People (DPP) v O' Shea*[112]:

> 'the judge would preside, ensure that all conditions for a fair and proper trial of that nature are complied with, decide all matters deemed to be matters of law, and direct the jury as to the legal principles and rules they are to observe and apply; and in which the jury, constituted in a manner calculated to ensure the achievement of the proper exercise of their functions, would be the arbiters, under the governance of the judge, of all disputed issues of fact and, in particular, the issue of guilt or innocence.'

Any issue as to the admissibility of evidence is a matter for the trial judge: *People (DPP) v Conroy*[113].

Judiciary

Article 34.1

> 'Justice shall be administered in Courts established by law by judges appointed in the manner provided by this Constitution…'

Independence of Judiciary: Article 35.2

> 'All judges shall be independent in the exercise of their judicial functions and subject only to this Constitution and the law.'

---

112 [1982] IR 384
113 [1986] IR 460

The independence of the judiciary refers to the autonomy to perform judicial functions free of interference and influence of the Oireachtas and other external pressures.

State (DPP) v Walsh[114]

> 'Article 35.2 is a solemn recognition that the judiciary shall be free to act as justice requires.'

Safeguards to protect the independence of the judiciary:

1. The Oireachtas must not interfere with matters pending before the Courts

Buckley v Attorney General[115]

O' Byrne J:

> 'The effect of [Arts. 34 to 37], inclusive, is to vest in the Courts the exclusive right to determine justiciable controversies between citizens or between a citizen or citizens, as the case may be, and the State.....The substantial effect of the [Sinn Féin Funds Act 1947] is that the dispute is determined by the Oireachtas and the Court is required and directed by the Oireachtas to dismiss the plaintiffs' claim without any hearing and without forming any opinion as to the rights of the respective parties to the dispute. In our opinion this is clearly repugnant to the provisions of the Constitution, as being an unwarrantable interference by the Oireachtas with the operations of the Courts in a purely judicial domain.'

2. The Oireachtas is prevented from introducing legislation to retrospectively reverse or interfere with decisions of the Court

114 [1981] IR 412
115 [1950] IR 67

Howard v Commissioner for Public Works (No. 3)[116]

Lynch J:

> 'To attempt to do so would contravene the constitutional separation of powers of Government between the various organs of State established by the Constitution in that the...Oireachtas would be trespassing on and into the judicial domain.'

However it is permissible for the Oireachtas to introduce legislation to change the law, the subject matter of previous litigation, provided any such legislation does not contravene the rights of parties to the proceedings: *Pine Valley Developments Ltd v Minister for the Environment*[117]

3. Selection of Punishment

- *Re Haughey*[118]

> 'The guilt or innocence of an accused can only be determined by a Court'

- *Deaton v Attorney General*[119]

O' Dalaigh CJ:

> '[T]he selection of punishment is an integral part of the administration of justice' and accordingly 'which of the alternative penalties prescribed by the section is proper to be imposed is, together with the issue of the guilt of the accused, a matter to be determined by the Court that tries him.'

116 [1994] 3 IR 394
117 [1987] IR 23
118 [1971] IR 217
119 [1963] IR 170, (1963) 98 ILTR 99

Note also *State (Sheerin) v Kennedy*[120], *State (O) v O' Brien*[121].

However it is permissible for the Oireachtas to prescribe:

- fixed penalties and minimum and maximum penalties for offences: *Deaton v Attorney General*[122],
- general parameters within which a sentence is to be imposed: *Osmanovic v DPP*[123],
- mandatory penalties: *State (O' Rourke) v Kelly*[124]; *Whelan & Lynch v Minister for Justice Equality and Law Reform*[125].

4. A judge's pay cannot be reduced while in office: Article 35.5

Article 35.5 ensures that a judge will not anticipate a reduction in pay if a particular decision is reached.

O' Byrne v Minister for Finance[126]

Maguire CJ:

> 'The purpose of [Article 35.5] is to safeguard the independence of judges.'

However necessary reductions can be made in respect of:

- the imposition of taxes, levies or other charges that are imposed by law on persons generally or persons belonging to a particular class,

[120] [1966] IR 379
[121] [1971] IR 42
[122] [1963] IR 170, (1963) 98 ILTR 99
[123] [2006] IESC 50
[124] [1983] IR 58
[125] [2010] IESC 34
[126] [1959] IR 1, (1960) 94 ILTR 11

- ◦ reductions in the public interest 'where such reductions have been or are made by law to the remuneration of persons belonging to classes of persons whose remuneration is paid out of public money.'

5. Removal of judge

A judge can only be removed from office for stated misbehaviour or incapacity, and then only upon resolutions passed by Dáil Éireann and by Seanad Éireann calling for his removal: Article 35.4.1

Article 35.4.1 ensures that a judge will not anticipate a removal from office if a particular decision is reached.

Note: *Sheedy Affair; Curtin v Dáil Éireann*[127]

6. Contempt of Court Proceedings can be dealt with summarily by a judge.

- *State (DPP) v Walsh*[128]

> '...implicit in the guarantee under Article 35.2 of independence to judges in the discharge of their judicial function, is a recognition that such judges must be free and independent to act summarily, if necessary to protect their judicial proceedings against criminal acts which are designed to interfere with the course of justice.'

- *Murphy v British Broadcasting Corporation*[129]

McKenchnie J:

> 'Under the separation of powers within our Constitution, Courts are not only entrusted but are mandated to deliver

[127] [2006] IESC S14
[128] [1981] IR 412
[129] [2005] 3 IR 336

justice and for that purpose judges have a constitutional safeguard of independence. Their capacity to achieve this would be seriously inhibited if they could not master their own destiny.'

7. A judge has absolute privilege when acting in his/her judicial capacity.

Note: *Byrne v Ireland*[130].

8. A judge should not be liable for the costs of judicial review proceedings.

McIlwraith v Fawsitt[131]

Finlay CJ:

'... under no circumstances should the High Court upon application for judicial review with regard to either a decision of a District Justice or of a Circuit Court judge award costs to a successful applicant in a case where there is no question of impropriety or mala fides on the part of the judge concerned and where he has not sought to defend an order which apparently is invalid.'

Note: *O'Connor v Carroll*[132].

9. No judge shall be eligible to be a member of either House of the Oireachtas or to hold any other office or position of emolument: Article 35.3.

130 [1972] IR 241

131 [1990] 1 IR 343, [1990] ILRM 1

132 [1999] 2 IR 160

7

President

Article 12

Article 12.1

> 'There shall be a President of Ireland (*Uachtarán na hÉireann*), hereinafter called the President, who shall take precedence over all other persons in the State and who shall exercise and perform the powers and functions conferred on the President by this Constitution and by law.'

Article 12 of the Constitution sets out, *inter alia*, the following matters:

- Procedure for the nomination of candidates for the presidency;
- Procedure for the conduct of presidential elections;
- Particulars and formalities relating to the office of President.

Functions and Powers

The President is not answerable to either House of the Oireachtas or to any Court for the exercise and performance of the powers and functions of the office of President[133].

However, the President may be impeached for stated misbehaviour[134].

In addition, any powers and functions vested in the President can only be exercised and performed by him on the advice of the Government except where the Constitution provides that he can act in his absolute discretion or after consultation with the Council of State[135].

Article	Functions and Powers
13.1	The President shall: • Appoint the Taoiseach on the nomination of Dáil Éireann • Appoint the other members of the Government on the nomination of the Taoiseach with the previous approval of Dáil Éireann • Accept the resignation or terminate the appointment of any member of the Government on the advice of the Taoiseach

(Continued)

[133] Article 13.8
[134] Article 12.10
[135] Article 13.9

(*Continued*)

Article	Functions and Powers
13.2	Dáil Éireann shall be summoned and dissolved by the President on the advice of the Taoiseach and the President may, in his absolute discretion, refuse to dissolve Dáil Éireann on the advice of a Taoiseach who has ceased to retain the support of a majority in the Dáil. The President may convene a meeting of either or both of the Houses of the Oireachtas at any time after consultation with the Council of State.
13.3	Every Bill passed or deemed to have been passed by both Houses of the Oireachtas requires the signature of the President for its enactment and the President shall promulgate every law made by the Oireachtas.
13.4 and 13.5	The President is the commander in chief of the defence forces. The exercise of the supreme command of the defence forces is regulated by law and all commissioned officers of the defence forces hold their commissions from the President.

(Continued)

(Continued)

Article	Functions and Powers
13.6	The President has a right of pardon and the power to commute or remit punishment imposed by any Court exercising criminal jurisdiction. However the power of commutation or remission may also be conferred by law on other authorities. In this regard it should be noted that Section 23(1) of the Criminal Justice Act 1951 provides that: 'Except in capital cases, the Government may commute or remit, in whole or in part, any punishment imposed by a Court exercising criminal jurisdiction, subject to such conditions as they may think proper.'
13.7	The President may, after consultation with the Council of State and having received approval from the Government: • Communicate with the Houses of the Oireachtas by message or address on any matter of national or public importance. • Address a message to the Nation at any time on any such matter.

(Continued)

(Continued)

Article	Functions and Powers
26	The President may, after consultation with the Council of State, refer a bill (save for money bills, a bill containing a proposal to amend the Constitution, or a bill the time for the consideration of which by SeanadÉireann had been abridged under Article 24) to the Supreme Court for a decision as to the constitutionality of the bill or part thereof. The President must decline to sign a bill in every case in which the Supreme Court decides that any provision of a Bill is repugnant to the Constitution. Once the Supreme Court has declared a bill Constitutional under the Article 26 procedure no challenge can be made on the constitutional validity of the resulting act thereafter[136]. The ratio decidendi of a Supreme Court decision in an Article 26 reference is binding on the lower courts: *Re O' Laighleis*[137], *The State (Lynch) v Cooney*[138].

(Continued)

136 Article 34.3.3
137 [1960] IR 93, (1961) 95 ILTR 92
138 [1982] IR 337, [1983] ILRM 89

(Continued)

Article	Functions and Powers
27	A majority of the members of the Seanad and not less than one-third of the members of the Dáil may, by joint petition addressed to the President, request the President to decline to sign and promulgate as a law any Bill (other than a Bill containing a proposal for the amendment of this Constitution) on the ground that the Bill contains a proposal of such national importance that the will of the people thereon ought to be ascertained. Where the President decides that the bill contains a proposal of such national importance that the will of the people thereon ought to be ascertained the Bill shall not be signed into law until the proposal has been approved by: • people at a Referendum within a period of eighteen months from the date of the President's decision or • resolution of Dáil Éireann passed within the said period after a dissolution and reassembly of Dáil Éireann

Presidential Commission[139]

The Presidential Commission will exercise and perform the powers and functions conferred on the President in the event of the absence of the President, or his temporary

[139] Article 14 of Bunreacht na hÉireann

or permanent incapacity or in the event of his death, resignation, removal from office, or failure to exercise and perform the powers and functions of his office. It consists of The Chief Justice, The Chairman of Dáil Éireann (An Ceann Comhairle), and Chairman of Seanad Éireann.

Council of State[140]

The Council of State aids and counsels the President on all matters on which the President may consult the said Council in relation to the exercise and performance by him of his powers and functions.

The Council of State consists of:

- Ex-officio members (the Taoiseach, the Tánaiste, the Chief Justice, the President of the High Court, the Chairman of Dáil Éireann, the Chairman of Seanad Éireann, and the Attorney General)
- Former Presidents, Taoisigh or Chief Justices able and willing to act as a member of the Council of State
- Up to seven persons appointed by the President as Council members.

[140] Articles 31 and 32 of Bunreacht na hÉireann

8

Attorney General

The position of Attorney General is governed by Article 30 of the Constitution and legislation (including, in particular, the Ministers and Secretaries Act 1924). Article 30.1 states that:

> 'There shall be an Attorney General who shall be the adviser of the Government in matters of law and legal opinion, and shall exercise and perform all such powers, functions and duties as are conferred or imposed on him by this Constitution or by law.'

Functions of the Attorney General

The main functions of the Attorney General are as follows:

- Legal advice (Advisory Counsel);
- Legislative drafting (Parliamentary Counsel);
- Litigation, conveyancing and other transactional practices (Chief State Solicitors Office);
- Statute law revision and consolidation (Statute Law Revision Unit).

In addition the following functions are conferred on the Attorney General:

Prosecution of Offences

Article 30.3 provides that:

> 'All crimes and offences prosecuted in any Court constituted under Article 34 of this Constitution other than a Court of summary jurisdiction shall be prosecuted in the name of the People and at the suit of the Attorney General or some other person authorised in accordance with law to act for that purpose.'

The authority to prosecute in respect of criminal offences, originally vested in the Attorney General under s 9 of the Criminal Justice (Administration) Act 1924, has been transferred to the Director of Public Prosecutions under s 3 of the Prosecution of Offences Act 1974.

Enforcement of Public Rights

The Attorney General has a duty in the enforcement of public rights. Section 6(1) of the Ministers and Secretaries Act 1924 refers to 'the assertion and protection of public rights'.

- *Moore v Attorney General*[141]

Kennedy CJ:

> '...[the Attorney General is] the legal representative of the public....in all litigation in the courts....in which the public may be involved as a party interested, whether as plaintiff or defendant, or otherwise.'

141 [1930] IR 417

- *Attorney General and Minister for Justice v Dublin United Tramways Limited*[142]

Maguire P:

> '...[the Attorney General has] authority to assert the rights of the public by action in the courts.'

Campus Oil v Minister for Industry and Energy (No. 2)[143]
Keane J:

> 'I am satisfied that the appropriate person to assert and defend the public interest....is the Attorney General.'

The Attorney General however does not have an exclusive role in the enforcement of public rights and in *Society for the Protection of Unborn Children (Ireland) Limited v Coogan*[144] Walsh J declared that "every member of the public has an interest in seeing that the fundamental law of the State is not defeated."

In addition, where a member of the public seeks to enforce a public right but lacks *locus standi* to do so he can apply to the Attorney General to join in the proceedings 'at the relation of' the member of the public in a 'relator action.'

Guardian of Constitution

Society for the Protection of Unborn Children (Ireland) Limited v Coogan[145]

142 [1939] IR 590, (1940) 74 ILTR 46
143 [1983] IR 88, [1984] ILRM 45
144 [1989] IR 734
145 [1989] IR 734

Walsh J:

> 'It is also clear that the Attorney General by virtue of his constitutional office also has cast upon him in the appropriate case the duty of defending the Constitution and vindicating the rights conferred or guaranteed by it.'

Note also: *Attorney General v X*[146].

Miscellaneous Functions

- The Attorney General addresses the Constitutionality of bills in Article 26 proceedings.
- The Attorney General must be a notice party under Order 60 Rules 1-3 of the Rules of the Superior Courts 1986 in respect of proceedings challenging the constitutional validity of legislation and where important issues of constitutional interpretation are raised.
- Endorsement of warrants of extradition under the Extradition (Amendment) Act 1987.

Independence

The Attorney General is nominated by the Taoiseach and appointed by the President.[147] However the Attorney General must not be a member of Government[148] and must be independent in the exercise of his functions.

- *McLoughlin v Minister for Social Welfare*[149]

---

146 [1992] 1 IR 1, [1992] ILRM 401, [1992] 2 CMLR 277
147 Article 30.2
148 Article 30.4
149 [1958] IR 1

Kingsmill Moore J:

> 'It was quite clear that the Attorney General is in no way the servant of the Government but is put into an independent position. He is a great officer of State, with grave responsibilities of a quasi-judicial as well as of an executive nature. The provision for his voluntary or forced resignation seem to recognise that it may be his business to adopt a line antagonistic to the government, and such a difference of opinion has to be resolved by his ceasing to hold an independent position. He is specifically excluded from being a member of the government, which again underlines his independent position.'

- *Attorney General v X*[150]

Costello J:

> 'Provision is made in the Constitution for the office of Attorney General. He is legal adviser to the Government. But in addition the Constitution imposes on him duties which he must fulfil independently of the Government… the Attorney General is an especially appropriate person to invoke the jurisdiction of the court in order to vindicate and defend the right to life of the unborn.'

- *Attorney General v Hamilton (No. 1)*[151]

McCarthy J:

> 'In my view, the nature of the office of the Attorney General charges him with the duty to enforce the Constitution whether it be in the protection of the unprotected, as in *Attorney General v X* or in a claim of public right, or otherwise. It follows…that, if the Attorney General

---

150 [1992] 1 IR 1, [1992] ILRM 401, [1992] 2 CMLR 277
151 [1993] 2 IR 250, [1993] ILRM 81

considers that the conduct of the inquiry involves a possible constitutional breach, he is entitled, in his own right, to invoke the jurisdiction of the courts. Independence of function in this context has its duties as well as its rights. … Because of his functions, having regard to the provisions for his resignation or the termination of his appointment under Article 30, he must be presumed to be acting with at least the tacit consent of the Government.'

9

Constitutional Rights

Personal Rights

Personal rights are governed by Articles 40-44 of the Constitution.

Restrictions

The rights protected by Articles 40-44 are not absolute.

Ryan v Attorney General[152]

Kenny J "none of the personal rights of the citizen are unlimited."

1. Proportionality Test

In determining whether a restriction on fundamental rights is constitutional the Courts adopt a proportionality test.

Heaney v Ireland[153]

152 [1965] IR 294
153 [1994] 3 IR 593

Costello J:

'The objective of the impugned provision must be of sufficient importance to warrant overriding a Constitutionally protected right. It must relate to concerns pressing and substantial in a free and democratic society. The means chosen must pass a proportionality test. They must:—

(a) be rationally connected to the objective and not be arbitrary, unfair or based on irrational considerations;

(b) impair the right as little as possible; and

(c) be such that their effects on rights are proportional to the objective.'

2. Conflict of Constitutional Rights

In addition, constitutional rights can be restricted in the event of a conflict of Constitutional rights.

The People (Director of Public Prosecutions) v Shaw[154]

Kenny J:

'There is a hierarchy of Constitutional rights and, when a conflict arises between them, that which ranks higher must prevail....When a conflict of Constitutional rights arises it must be resolved by having regard to (a) the terms of the Constitution and (b) the ethical values which all Christians living in the State acknowledge and accept and (c) the main tenets of our system of Constitutional parliamentary democracy...'

[154] [1982] IR 1

Remedies for Breach of Constitutional Rights

A plaintiff can claim:

- A declaratory order confirming that the plaintiff's Constitutional rights have been contravened;
- An injunction to restrain a breach of Constitutional rights or to make provision for Constitutional rights;
- Damages for a breach of Constitutional rights including ordinary compensatory damages, aggravated damages and punitive or exemplary damages: *Conway v INTO*[155].

Rights under European Convention on Human Rights

In addition to Constitutional rights an Irish citizen has rights under the European Convention on Human Rights, which was incorporated into Irish law by the European Convention on Human Rights Act 2003.

A claim for breach of Constitutional rights can be made in conjunction with a claim for breach of equivalent rights under the Convention.

The rights protected by the European Convention on Human Rights are as follows:

Article 1: Respecting rights
Article 2: Right to life
Article 3: Prohibition of torture, ill-treatment
Article 4: Prohibition of slavery and forced labour
Article 5: Right to liberty and security
Article 6: Right to a fair trial
Article 7: No punishment without law

155 [1991] 2 IR 305, [1991] ILRM 497

Article 8: Right to respect for private and family life
Article 9: Freedom of thought, conscience and religion
Article 10: Freedom of expression
Article 11: Freedom of assembly and association
Article 12: Right to marriage
Article 13: Right to an effective remedy
Article 14: Prohibition of discrimination

The protocols to the Convention provide addition rights to include, *inter alia,* the right to peaceful enjoyment of one's possessions and the right to education.

10

Personal Rights Under Article 40.3

Article 40.3 of the Constitution provides that:

'1. The State guarantees in its laws to respect, and, as far as practicable, by its laws to defend and vindicate the personal rights of the citizen.

2. The State shall, in particular, by its laws protect as best it may from unjust attack and, in the case of injustice done, vindicate the life, person, good name, and property rights of every citizen.'

Specific Rights

Article 40.3.2 enumerates four specific rights, namely:

- The Right to Life
- The Right of the Person to Protection
- The Right to a Good Name
- Property Rights

Right to Life

G *v An Bord Uchtála*[156]

Walsh J:

> '[T]he right to life necessarily implies 'the right to be born, the right to preserve and defend, and to have preserved and defended that life and the right to maintain that life at a proper human standard in matters of food, clothing and habitation.'

The right to life however does not include a corresponding right to have one's life terminated.

Re a Ward of Court (withholding medical treatment) (No. 2)[157]

Hamilton CJ:

> 'As the process of dying is part, and an ultimate, inevitable consequence, of life, the right to life necessarily implies the right to have nature take its course and to die a natural death and, unless the individual concerned so wishes, not to have life artificially maintained by the provision of nourishment by abnormal artificial means, which have no curative effect and which is intended merely to prolong life.'

Protection of Person

The right of the person to protection has been pleaded sparingly before the Irish Courts.

---

156 [1980] IR 32, (1979) 113 ILTR 25
157 [1996] 2 IR 79, [1995] 2 ILRM 401

Right to a Good Name

In *Re Haughey*[158] it was recognised that the right to one's good name includes a right to adequately defend one's good name.

Property Rights

Property rights will be considered in full in chapter 16.

Un-enumerated Rights

Un-enumerated rights are personal rights which are not specified in the Constitution but have been recognised by the judiciary as implied fundamental rights Constitutionally protected under Article 40.3.1.

In *Ryan v Attorney General*[159] Kenny J held that such rights arise from 'the Christian and democratic nature of the State' and that the use of the words 'in particular' in ss 2 indicate that 'the general guarantee in ss 1 must extend to rights not specified in Article 40.'

In *McGee v Attorney General*[160] Henchy J espoused that unspecified rights were derived from natural law principles and that, for the Courts to decide whether a right comes within the constitutional guarantee specified in ss 1 'it must be shown that it is a right that inheres in the citizen in question by virtue of his human personality.'

In addition certain un-enumerated rights have been held to arise, by necessary inference, from rights expressly identified in the Constitution.

---

[158] [1971] IR 217

[159] [1965] IR 294

[160] [1974] IR 284, (1975) 109 ILTR 29

While a number of un-enumerated rights have been recognise by the Courts, Keane CJ in *O' T v B*[161] cautioned that 'some degree of judicial restraint is called for in identifying new rights of this nature.'

Note also: *TD v Minister for Education*[162].
The schedule to this chapter outlines the un-enumerated rights which have been recognised by the Courts.

161 [1998] 2 IR 321
162 2001 4 IR 259 (Supreme Court), 2000 2 ILRM 321 (High Court)

Right: Privacy

Recognition of the Right	*McGee v Attorney General*[163] Budd J. "the right to privacy is universally recognised and accepted" and "the matter of marital relationships must rank as one of the most important matters in the realm of privacy" Walsh J "it is outside the authority of the State to endeavour to intrude into the privacy of the husband and wife relationship for the sake of imposing a code of private morality upon the husband and wife which they do not desire." • *Digital Rights Ireland v Minister for Communications & Ors*[164] – companies have a right to privacy
Right is not absolute	*McGee v Attorney General*[165] Walsh J. "The private morality of its citizens does not justify intervention by the State into the activities of those citizens unless and until the common good requires it" *Norris v AG*[166] O' Higgins CJ "A right of privacy…can never be absolute. There are many acts done in private which the State is entitled to condemn, whether such be done by an individual on his own or with another. *Foy v An t-Ard Chlaraitheoir & Ors*[167] McKechnie J. "Everyone as a member of society has the right to human dignity, and with individual personalities, has

(Continued)

[163] [1974] IR 284, (1975) 109 ILTR 29
[164] [2010] IEHC 221
[165] [1974] IR 284, (1975) 109 ILTR 29
[166] [1984] IR 36
[167] [2007] IEHC 470

Right: Privacy (*Continued*)

	the right to develop his being as he sees fit; subject only to the most minimal of State interference being essential for the convergence of the common good. Together with human freedom, a person, subject to the acquired rights of others, should be free to shape his personality in the way best suited to his person and to his life." • Surveillance and interception of communications *Kennedy v Ireland*[168] Hamilton P. "the dignity and freedom of an individual in a democratic society cannot be ensured if his communications of a private nature, be they written or telephonic, are deliberately, consciously and unjustifiably intruded upon and interfered with" however "an individual must accept the fact that in certain circumstance the exigencies of the common good may require and justify such intrusion and interference." • Journalistic Intrusion *Herrity v Associated Newspapers*[169] Dunne J "....I think that cases in which the right to privacy will prevail over the right to freedom of expression may well be far and few between"

(*Continued*)

[168] [1987] IR 587, [1988] ILRM 472
[169] [2008] IEHC 249

Right: Privacy (*continued*)

	Note also *X v Flynn & Ors*[170] and *M. Drury & Ors*[171] on journalistic intrusion • *Re a Ward of Court* (No. 2)[172] - right to privacy includes a right to refuse medical treatment but does not include a right to have life terminated.

Right: Earn a Livelihood

Recognition of the Right	*Murtagh Properties v Cleary*[173] Kenny J (citing Article 45 Directives Principles of Social Policy) "[The Constitution guarantees that] citizens.... may through their occupation find the means of making reasonable provision for their domestic needs" • The right to earn a livelihood can be enforced against private individuals as well as the State: *Parsons v Kavanagh*[174], *Lovett v Gogan*[175]
Right is not absolute	*Attorney General and Minister for Posts and Telegraphs v Paperlink*[176] Costello J "[The right to earn a livelihood] is not an absolute one, however, and it may be subject to legitimate legal restrains." • The right to earn a livelihood can be subject to restrictions based on the exigencies of the common good:

(*Continued*)

170 19 May 1994, unreported, High Court
171 [1994] 2 IR 8
172 [1996] 2 IR 79, [1995] 2 ILRM 401
173 [1972] IR 330
174 [1990] ILRM 560
175 [1995] 3 IR 132
176 [1984] ILRM 373

Right: **Earn a Livelihood (*Continued*)**

	Landers v Attorney General[177] *Cafolla v O' Malley & Attorney General*[178] *Hand v Dublin Corporation*[179] *Shanley v Galway Corporation*[180] *Kenny v Dental Council*[181] • *Cox v Ireland*[182] - a restriction on the right to earn a livelihood must be proportionate to the objective sought to be achieved.

Right: Communicate

Recognition of the Right	*Attorney General and Minister for Posts and Telegraphs v Paperlink*[183] Costello J. "As the right to communicate is the exercise of such a basic human faculty....a right to communicate must inhere in the citizen by virtue of his human personality and must be guaranteed by the Constitution."
Right is not absolute	*Attorney General and Minister for Posts and Telegraphs v Paperlink*[184] Costello J. "But the right to communicate is obviously not an absolute one. Laws may restrict the nature of the matter communicated (for example, by prohibiting the communication of confidential information or treasonable, blasphemous, obscene or defamatory matter) and laws may also restrict the mode of

(*Continued*)

177 (1973) 109 ILTR 1
178 [1985] IR 486
179 [1991] 1 IR 409
180 [1995] 1 IR 396
181 [2004] IEHC 29
182 [1992] 2 IR 503
183 [1984] ILRM 373
184 [1984] ILRM 373

Right: Communicate (*Continued*)

	communication (for example by prohibiting communication by advertisement contrary to the planning code or by radio contrary to wireless telegraphy regulations)." *Murphy v Independent Television and Radio Commission*[185] Barrington J. "It is established in all the relevant decided cases that the personal rights protected by [Article 40.3.1] are not absolute and that their exercise may be regulated in the common good…. It is not obvious to me that a restriction on religious advertising is not a reasonable restriction in the interest of the common good on this particular form of exercise of the right to communicate." *Kearney v Minister for Justice*[186] – Prison Rule 63 (reading of letters to and from prisoners) was justified to maintain prison security

Right: **Bodily Integrity**

Recognition of the Right	*Ryan v Attorney General*[187] Kenny J. "In my opinion, one of the personal rights of the citizen protected by the general guarantee [in Article 40.3.1] is the right to bodily integrity" Kenny J. described the right as follows: "I understand the right to bodily integrity to mean that no mutilation of the body or any of its members may be carried out on any citizen under authority of the law except for the good of the whole body and that no process which is or may, as a matter of

(*Continued*)

[185] [1999] 1 IR 12, [1997] 2 ILRM 467 (HC), [1999] IR 29 (SC)
[186] [1986] IR 116
[187] [1965] IR 294

Right: Bodily Integrity (*Continued*)

	probability, be dangerous or harmful to the life or health of the citizens or any of them may be imposed (in the sense of being made compulsory) by an Act of the Oireachtas." • *People (DPP) v Tiernan*[188], *People (DPP) v JT*[189] - the right to bodily integrity can be enforced against private individuals as well as the State. • *Re A Ward of Court* (Withholding of Medical Treatment)[190] - the right to bodily integrity includes a right to consent to and refuse medical treatment. • *The State (Richardson) v The Governor of Mountjoy Prison*[191] Barrington J. "the State has failed in its duty under the Constitution and under the [Prison] Rules to protect the applicants health and to provide her with appropriate facilities to maintain proper standards of hygiene and cleanliness"
Right is not absolute	*State (C) v Frawley*[192] Finlay P. "I must construe the entire concept of torture, inhuman and degrading treatment and punishment as being not only evil in its consequences but evil in its purpose as well. It is most commonly inspired by revenge, retaliation, the creation of fear or improper interrogation. It is to me inconceivable to associate it with the necessary discharge of a duty to prevent self injury or self destruction"

188 [1988] IR 250, [1989] ILRM 149
189 (1984-1989) 3 Frewen 141
190 [1996] 2 IR 79
191 [1980] ILRM 82
192 [1976] IR 365

Right: Reasonable Access to a Solicitor

Recognition of the Right	*The People (DPP) v Healy*[193] Finlay CJ "such important and fundamental standard of fairness in the administration of justice as the right of access to a lawyer must be deemed to be constitutional in its origin, and ...to classify it as merely legal would be to undermine its importance and the completeness of the protection of it which the courts are obliged to give" The access to a solicitor must be in private: *DPP v Finnegan*[194]
Right is not absolute	*Lavery v The Member in Charge Carrickmacross Garda Station*[195] O' Flaherty J "The solicitor is not entitled to be present at the interviews. Neither was it open to the respondent, or his solicitor, to prescribe the manner by which the interviews might be conducted, or where." The Gardai are not prohibited from questioning a detainee pending the arrival of a Solicitor: *The People v Buck*[196]

Right: **Access to the Courts**

Recognition of the Right	*MacAuley v Minister for Posts and Telegraphs*[197] Kenny J. "That there is a right to have recourse to the High Court to defend and vindicate a legal right and that it is one of the personal rights of the citizen included

(Continued)

[193] [1990] 2 IR 73
[194] 15 July 1997, unreported, Court of Criminal Appeal
[195] [1999] 2 IR 390
[196] [2002] 2 IR 268
[197] [1966] IR 345

Right: Access to the Courts (*Continued*)

	in the general guarantee of Article 40.3 seems to me to be a necessary inference from Article 34.3.1…" *O' Brien v Manufacturing Engineering Company Ltd*[198] Walsh J. "[there is] a right to litigate claims, which are justifiable in law" • *Article 26 and ss 5 and 10 of the Illegal Immigrants (Trafficking) Bill 1999*[199] - non-nationals have a right of access to the courts.
Right is not absolute	The right of access to the courts can restricted by the imposition of statutory limitation periods: *O' Brien v Manufacturing Engineering Company Limited*[200] - a limitation period is valid where it gives the plaintiff sufficient opportunity to determine whether there is a cause of action and to institute proceedings. *Article 26 and ss 5 and 10 of the Illegal Immigrants (Trafficking) Bill 1999*[201] Keane CJ "The legislature is not obliged to choose the longest possible period that might be thought consistent with the policy objective concerned. However, in exercising that discretion the legislature must not undermine or compromise a substantive right guaranteed by the Constitution such as the right of access to the courts. Where a limitation period is so restrictive as to render access to the courts impossible or excessively difficult it may be considered unreasonable … and therefore unconstitutional."

(*Continued*)

198 [1973] IR 334
199 [2000] 2 IR 360
200 [1973] IR 334
201 [2000] 2 IR 360

Right: Access to the Courts (*Continued*)

	• Note the following caselaw on statutory limitation periods: *O' Brien v Keogh*[202]; *Tuohy v Courtney*[203]; *Cahill v Sutton*[204]; *Morgan v Park Developments Limited*[205]; *Hegarty v O' Loughran*[206]; *White v Dublin Corporation*[207] • *Blehein v The Minister for Health*[208] – the granting of leave for judicial review only on proof of acting in bad faith or without reasonable care was an impermissible restriction on the right of access to the Courts.

Right: Access to Legal Aid

Recognition of the Right	*State (Healy) v Donoghue*[209] Henchy J. recognised a right to legal aid in criminal matters "A person who has been convicted and deprived of his liberty as a result of a prosecution which, because of his poverty, he has had to bear without legal aid has reason to complain that he has been meted out less than his constitutional due. This is particularly true if the absence of legal aid is compounded by factors such as a grave or complex charge; or ignorance, illiteracy, immaturity or other conditions rendering the accused incompetent to cope properly with the prosecution; or an

(*Continued*)

202 [1972] IR 144
203 [1994] 3 IR 1
204 [1980] IR 269
205 [1983] ILRM 156
206 [1990] 1 IR 148
207 [2004] 1 IR 545
208 [2008] IESC 40
209 [1976] IR 325

Right: Access to Legal Aid (*Continued*)

	inability, because of detentional restraint, to find and produce witnesses; or simply the fumbling incompetence that may occur when an accused is precipitated into the public glare and alien complexity of courtroom procedures, and is confronted with the might of a prosecution backed by the State. As the law stands, a legal-aid certificate is the shield provided against such an unjust attack."
Right is not absolute	• *State (O) v Daly*[210] O' Higgins CJ the constitutional right to legal aid in criminal trials does not extend to "the earlier or ancillary stages of the criminal proceedings." • There is no general right to civil legal aid: *Magee v Farrell*[211] Finnegan J. "A right to legal representation does not carry with it a right to State funded legal aid. Where, however, the liberty of the individual is in issue before the Criminal Courts there is an entitlement to State funded legal aid." Note the following caselaw on civil legal aid: *O' Shaughnessy v Attorney General*[212]; *MacGairbhith v Attorney General*[213]; *MC v Legal Aid Board*[214]; *Stevenson v Landy*[215]; *Kirwan v Minister for Justice*[216]; *McBrearty v Morris*[217];

210 [1977] IR 312
211 [2009] 2 ILRM 453
212 16 February 1971, unreported, High Court
213 [1991] IR 412
214 [1991] 2 IR 43
215 10 February 1993, unreported, High Court
216 [1994] 2 IR 417, [1994] 1 ILRM 444
217 13 May 2003, unreported, High Court

Right: Right to Fair Procedures

Recognition of the Right	*Re Haughey*[218] O' Dalaigh CJ "Article 40, s. 3, of the Constitution is a guarantee to the citizen of basic fairness of procedures. The Constitution guarantees such fairness, and it is the duty of the Court to underline that the words of Article 40, s. 3, are not political shibboleths but provide a positive protection for the citizen and his good name." *Garvey v Ireland*[219] O' Higgins CJ "...[In Article 40.3] there is guaranteed to every citizen whose rights be affected by decisions taken by others the right to fair and just procedures. This means that under the Constitution powers cannot be exercised unjustly or unfairly." *McDonald v Bord na gCon*[220] Walsh J "In the context of the Constitution natural justice might be more appropriately termed constitutional justice and must be understood to import more than the two well established principles that no man shall be judge in his own cause and audi alteram partem" • Nemo Iudex (no bias rule) *Dublin Well Woman Centre Ltd v Ireland*[221] Denham J. "The concept of bias developed through cases considering material interest. It also arose in cases on pre-judgment, prior involvement, and personal

(*Continued*)

[218] [1971] IR 217
[219] [1981] IR 75
[220] [1965] IR 217
[221] [1995] ILRM 408

Right: Right to Fair Procedures (*Continued*)

	attitudes and beliefs. There are two fundamental streams of thought within this wider concept. First, that there should be no actual bias, i.e. a subjective test. And secondly, that there should be no reasonable apprehension that there is bias, i.e. the objective test." • Audi Alterem Partem (hear the other side) *Re Haughey*[222] recognised that this includes the following: "(*a*) that he should be furnished with a copy of the evidence which reflected on his good name; (*b*) that he should be allowed to cross-examine, by counsel, his accuser or accusers; (*c*) that he should be allowed to give rebutting evidence; and (d) that he should be permitted to address, again by counsel, the Committee in his own defence."
Right is not absolute	The right to fair procedures is subject to limitation in certain circumstances: the legislative process (*Cassidy v Minister for Industry and Commerce*[223]; *Gorman v Minister for the Environment*[224]); major policy decisions (*Bushell v Secretary of the Environment*)[225]; countervailing factors (*O'Callaghan v Commissioners of Public Works*[226]); where the individual interest affected is too trivial; suspension from employment pending a full hearing; private transactions and arrangements save for employment disputes.

(*Continued*)

[222] [1971] IR 217
[223] [1978] IR 297
[224] [2001] 1 IR 306
[225] [1981] AC 75
[226] [1985] ILRM 364

Right: Right to Fair Procedures (*Continued*)

	Exception to the No Bias Rule Necessity: *O' Neill v Beaumont Hospital Board*[227]; *O'Byrne v Minister for Finance*[228]; Waiver: *Corrigan v Irish Land Commission*[229]

Right: To know one's natural mother

Recognition of the Right	*I. O'T v B*[230] Hamilton CJ "The right to know the identity of ones natural mother is a basic right flowing from the natural and special relationship which exists between a mother and her child...."
Right is not absolute	*I. O'T v B*[231] Hamilton CJ "[the right to know the identity of their respective natural mothers is not] an absolute or qualified right: its exercise may be restricted by the constitutional rights of others, and by the requirement of the common good."

Right: Travel

Recognition of the Right	*Ryan v Attorney General*[232] Kenny J. recognised a "right to free movement within the State" *State (M) v Attorney General*[233] Finlay P. recognised "a right to travel outside the State"

(*Continued*)

227 [1990] ILRM 419
228 [1959] IR 1, (1960) 94 ILTR 11
229 [1997] IR 317
230 [1998] 2 IR 321
231 [1998] 2 IR 321
232 [1965] IR 294
233 [1979] IR 73

Right: Travel (*Continued*)

Right is not absolute	*State (M) v Attorney General*[234] Finlay P. The right to travel is subject to "obvious and justified restrictions" *X v Attorney General*[235] McCarthy J. "[the right to travel] cannot be curtailed because of a particular intent."

Right: Rights of the non-marital child and its mother

Recognition of the Right	*State (Nicolaou) v An Bord Uchtala*[236]: an unmarried mother has a right to the care and custody of her child under Article 40.3 *G v An Bord Uchtala*[237]: The Child has certain unenumerated rights. O' Higgins CJ "Having been born, the child has the right to be fed and to live, to be reared and educated, to have the opportunity of working and of realising his or her full personality and dignity as a human being." In *M v M*[238] Murphy J confirmed that such rights extended to non-marital children

234 [1979] IR 73
235 [1992] 1 IR 1, [1992] ILRM 401, [1992] 2 CMLR 277
236 [1966] IR 567, (1986) 102 ILTR 1
237 [1980] IR 32, (1979) 113 ILTR 25
238 2 December 1982, unreported, High Court

Right: To Marry and Procreate

Recognition of the Right	• Recognition of a Right to Marry *Ryan v Attorney General*[239] *McGee v Attorney General*[240] • Recognition of a Right to Beget Children *Murray v Attorney General*[241]
Right is not absolute	• *Murray v Attorney General*[242] Costello J. "The reasonable requirements of the prison service would not, in my judgment, permit the exercise by all married prisoners of their right to beget children, and so the concession made in this connection was properly made. This means that the fact of imprisonment does not in itself amount to an unconstitutional infringement of a prisoner's rights...it would place unreasonable demands on the prison service to require prison authorities to make facilities available within the confines of the prison to enable all prisoners who fall within this category to exercise their right to beget children."

[239] [1965] IR 294
[240] [1974] IR 284, (1975) 109 ILTR 29
[241] [1985] IR 532
[242] [1985] IR 532

11

Equality: Article 40.1

Article 40 of the Constitution provides that:

> 'All citizens shall, as human persons, be equal before the law. This shall not be held to mean that the State shall not in its enactments have due regard to differences of capacity, physical and moral and of social function.'

Invocation

Article 40.1 can be invoked against the State and State organs. It would appear that it does not have horizontal effect and cannot be invoked against private parties.

The Equality Tribunal v Portmarnock Golf Club & Ors[243]
O' Higgins J:

> '...Article 40.1 of the Constitution guarantees process equality and does not impose obligations on citizens in their private relations.'

243 [2005] IEHC 235

Beneficiaries

The right to equality in Article 40.1 can only be invoked by citizens as 'human persons.'A body corporate cannot invoke it.

- *Quinn's Supermarket v Attorney General*[244]

Walsh J:

> '...under no possible construction of the Constitutional guarantee could a body corporate or any entity but a human being be considered to be a human person for the purpose of [Article 40.1].'

- *J & J Haire & Company Ltd & Ors v Min for Health & Ors*[245]

McMahon J:

> '[T]he equality protection under the Constitution extends to human persons only and may not be availed of by companies or other legal entities.'

In addition Article 40.1 prohibits discrimination relating to the essential attributes or characteristics of human beings such as race, ethnicity, colour, gender, sexual orientation and so on.

- *Re Article 26 and the Employment Equality Bill 1996*[246]

> 'The forms of discrimination which are, presumptively at least, prescribed by Article 40.1 are not particularised: manifestly, they would extend to classifications based on sex, race, language, religious or political opinions.'

---

244 [1972] IR 1
245 [2009] IEHC 562
246 [1997] 2 IR 321, [1997] 8 ELR 132

It does not relate to discrimination based on the commercial activities, career or profession of the citizen.

Quinn's Supermarket v Attorney General[247]
Walsh J.

> '[Article 40.1] refers to human persons for what they are themselves rather than their lawful activities, trades or pursuits.'

- *Murtagh Properties v Cleary*[248]

Kenny J:

> '[Article 40.1 relates to the citizens] attributes as human persons, those features which make them human beings. It is in my opinion nothing to do with their trading activities or with the conditions on which they are employed.'

- *Redmond v Minister for the Environment*[249]

Herbert J adopted a broader view of what constitutes an attribute of the human person and determined that classification or discrimination based on wealth may violate Article 40.1.

> 'A law which has the effect, even if totally unintended, of discriminating between human persons on the basis of money is an attack upon the dignity of those persons as human beings who do not have money.... The history of poverty and social deprivation in Ireland, but by no means exclusively in Ireland, demonstrates overwhelmingly the extent to which the essential dignity of persons as human beings is involved. In my judgment, this is

247 [1972] IR 1
248 [1972] IR 330
249 [2001] 4 IR 61

exactly the type of discrimination for which the framers of the first sentence of Article 40, section 1 of the Constitution were providing'.

Limited Right

The right to equality is not absolute.

- *Quinn's Supermarket v Attorney General*[250]

Walsh J:

> '...this provision is not a guarantee of absolute equality for all citizens in all circumstances but is a guarantee of equality as human persons and (as the Irish text of the Constitution makes quite clear) is a guarantee related to their dignity as human beings and a guarantee against any inequalities grounded upon an assumption, or indeed a belief, that some individual or individuals or classes of individuals, by reason of their human attributes or their ethnic or racial, social or religious background, are to be treated as the inferior or superior of other individuals in the community.'

- *De Burca & Anderson v Attorney General*[251]

Walsh J:

> 'Article 40 does not require identical treatment of all persons without recognition of differences in relevant circumstances but it forbids invidious or arbitrary discrimination.'

Any restriction on the right to equality must be reasonable and proportionate.

---

250 [1972] IR 1
251 [1976] IR 38, (1977) 111 ILTR 37

- *O' B v S*[252]

Walsh J:

> '[T]he distinctions or discrimination which the legislation creates must not be unjust, unreasonable or arbitrary and must, of course, be relevant to the legislation in question.'

- *Murphy v AG*[253]

Kenny J:

> '...inequality would not be set aside as repugnant to the Constitution....if any state of facts exist which may reasonably justify it.'

Difference in Treatment

A difference in treatment can be justified in the following circumstances:

1. The differential treatment is rational and reasonable and for legitimate legislative purpose

- *Brennan v Attorney General*[254]

Barrington J:

> '[T]he classification must be for a legitimate legislative purpose...it must be relevant to that purpose, and...each class must be treated fairly.'

The following categories of discrimination should be noted:

---

[252] [1984] IR 316, [1985] ILRM 86
[253] [1982] IR 241
[254] [1983] ILRM 449 (High Court), [1984] ILRM 355 (Supreme Court)

A. Gender

Gender based discrimination cannot be justified unless the proviso applies.

- *de Burca & Anderson v Attorney General*[255]

Classification based on gender was deemed unconstitutionally.

Walsh J:

> '...it is not open to the State to discriminate in its enactments between the persons who are subject to its laws solely upon the ground of the sex of those persons. If a reference is to be made to the sex of a person, then the purpose of the law that makes such a discrimination should be to deal with some physical or moral capacity or social function that is related exclusively or very largely to that sex only.'

Similarly in *W v W*[256] it was found that 'there can be no sex discrimination between equals.'

Note also: *Norris v Attorney*[257], *O' G v AG*[258], *Somjee v Minister for Justice*[259], *D v Ireland*[260]

B. Pedigree

Classification based on pedigree was held unconstitutional by the Supreme Court in *An Blascaod Mór Teo v Commissioner of Public Works*[261].

---

[255] [1976] IR 38, (1977) 111 ILTR 37

[256] [1993] 2 IR 476, [1993] ILRM 294

[257] [1984] IR 36

[258] [1985] ILRM 61

[259] [1981] ILRM 324

[260] 26 March 2010, unreported, High Court

[261] [2000] 1 IR 6

C. Age

Classification based on age was endorsed in *D v Residential Institutions Redress Review Committee*[262]. Murray CJ:

> 'Almost all legislation addressed to the regulation of society resorts to some form of classification. Age is frequently used as a classification of inclusion or exclusion for multitudes of legislative purposes. There is nothing in such classification, taken on its own, to suggest that it is invidious, unfair or in the legal sense discriminatory.'

2. Differences of Capacity, Physical and Moral and of Social Function

Article 40.1 provides that the guarantee of equality therein

> '...shall not be held to mean that the State shall not in its enactments have due regard to differences of capacity, physical and moral and of social function.'

Examples

- *Re Philip Clarke*[263]

Difference in treatment justified by the applicant's mental infirmity.

- *The State (Nicolaou) v An Bord Uachtála*[264]

Difference in treatment between a natural mother and a natural father in the adoption process was justified by a difference in parental capacity.

[262] [2009] IESC 59
[263] [1950] IR 235, (1951) 85 ILTR 119
[264] [1966] IR 567, (1986) 102 ILTR 1

- *Mhic Mhathuna v Ireland*[265]

Difference in treatment between single and married parents in tax and social welfare codes justified by the financial needs and circumstances of single parents.

3. Justification derived from other Constitutional safeguards

- *O' B v S*[266]

> 'Legislation which differentiates citizens or which discriminates between them does not need to be justified under the proviso if justification can be found in other provisions of the Constitution. Legislation, which is unjust, unreasonable or arbitrary, cannot be justified under any provision of the Constitution. Conversely, if legislation can be justified under one or more Articles of the Constitution, when read with all others, it cannot be held to be unjust within the meaning of the Article.'

In this case, the provision in the Succession Act 1965 that a non-marital child had no right to inherit on the intestacy of his natural father was justified in order to protect the institution of marriage.

- *De Burca & Anderson v Attorney General*[267]

The exemption of women from jury service was justified by the Constitutions recognition of the woman's and mother's role in the home

265 [1989] IR 504
266 [1984] IR 316, [1985] ILRM 86
267 [1976] IR 38, (1977) 111 ILTR 37

- *Dennehy v Minister for Social Welfare*[268] *and Lowth v Minister for Social Welfare*[269]

The Constitutional acknowledgement of the woman's role in the home was used to justify the provision of certain allowances to deserted wives but not deserted husbands.

- *Zappone & Gilligan v Revenue Commissioners*[270]

Difference in treatment between hetrosexual and same sex couples is justified by the meaning of marriage in Articles 41 and 42.

Proportionate Discrimination

A difference in treatment can only be permissible where it is proportionate to the objective.

Re Article 26 and the Employment Equality Bill 1996[271]

In this case, the Supreme Court adopted the following proportionality test:

> 'In considering the proportionality of the provision, the Court must ask;
>
> (a) Is it rationally designed to meet the objective of the legislation?
>
> (b) Does it intrude into constitutional rights as little as possible?
>
> (c) Is there a proportionality between the section…the objective of the legislation?'

268 26 July 1984, unreported, High Court
269 [1998] 4 IR 321, [1999] 1 ILRM 5
270 [2006] IEHC 404
271 [1997] 2 IR 321, [1997] 8 ELR 132

12

Freedom of Expression

Article 40.6.1 of the Constitution provides that:

> 'The State guarantees liberty for the exercise of the following rights, subject to public order and morality:
>
> i. The right of the citizens to express freely their convictions and opinions.
>
> The education of public opinion being, however, a matter of such grave import to the common good, the State shall endeavour to ensure that organs of public opinion, such as the radio, the press, the cinema, while preserving their rightful liberty of expression, including criticism of Government policy, shall not be used to undermine public order or morality or the authority of the State.
>
> The publication or utterance of blasphemous, seditious, or indecent matter is an offence which shall be punishable in accordance with law.'

In *Mahon v Kenna and Kennedy*[272] Fennelly J in the Supreme Court referred to Johnson P's recognition in the High Court of 'the importance of the right to freedom of expression in

---

[272] [2009] IESC 64

a democratic society' and 'the critical importance of a free press as an essential organ in a democratic society.'

Distinction from Right to Communicate

In *Murphy v Independent Television and Radio Commission*[273] Barrington J distinguished between the right to communicate in Article 40.3 and Freedom of Expression in Article 40.6.1. He referred to the right to communicate as 'the right to convey ones needs and emotions by words and gestures as well as by rational discourse' while the right to freedom of expression applies to public statements and 'is concerned with the public activities of the citizen in a democratic society.' It is a right 'not only to communicate opinions but also to communicate the fact on which these opinions are based.'

However in *Mahon v Post Publications Limited*[274] Fennelly J ruled that:

> 'Clearly, the Constitution, unequivocally guarantees both the right to express convictions and opinions and the right to communicate facts or information. These rights are inseparable. It matters little, at least for present purposes, which Article of the Constitution expresses the guarantee. The right of a free press to communicate information without let or restraint is intrinsic to a free and democratic society.'

Limitations

The right to freedom of expression is not absolute but is subject to public order, morality and state security.

[273] [1999] 1 IR 12
[274] [2007] IESC 15

State (Lynch) v Cooney[275]:

> '[T]he basis for any attempt to control must be according to the Constitution, the overriding considerations of public order and public morality.'

In *Murphy v Independent Television and Radio Commission*[276] Barrington J held that the right to freedom of expression 'can, in certain circumstances, be limited in the interests of the common good.'

The Courts apply a proportionality test and in *Murphy* Barrington J identified that:

> 'The real question is whether the limitation imposed upon the various constitutional rights is proportionate to the purpose which the Oireachtas wished to achieve.'

Note also. *Colgan v Independent Radio and Television Commission*[277], *Kearney v Minister for Justice*[278], *Holland v Governor of Portlaois Prison*[279]

1. Public Order and Security

An example of a restriction on freedom of expression is sedition (inciting another to violence) which is recognised as an offence under Article 40.6.1(i) of the Constitution and such offences are primarily governed by the Offences Against the State Act 1939.

[275] [1982] IR 337, [1983] ILRM 89
[276] [1999] 1 IR 12
[277] [2000] 2 IR 490, [1999] 1 ILRM 22
[278] [1986] IR 116
[279] [2004] 2 IR 573

2. Public Morality

Article 40.6.1 provides that 'the publication or utterance of blasphemous, seditious or indecent matter or material' is an offence.

Section 36 of the Defamation Act 2009 provides that blasphemy consists of publishing or uttering:

> '[M]atter that is grossly abusive or insulting in relation to matters held sacred by any religion, thereby causing outrage among a substantial number of the adherents of that religion[with an intention]by the publication or utterance of the matter concerned, to cause such outrage.'

The Censorship of Films Acts 1923-1992 permit the censorship of film where

> '[S]uch picture or some part thereof is unfit for general exhibition in public by reason of its being indecent, obscene or blasphemous or because the exhibition thereof in public would tend to inculcate principles contrary to public morality or would be otherwise subversive of public morality[280].'

The Video Recordings Acts 1989-1992 permit the censorship of video/DVD where any such work:

> '(i) would be likely to cause persons to commit a crime..., or
>
> (ii) would be likely to stir up hatred against a group of persons on account of their race, colour, nationality, religion, ethnic or national origins, membership of the travelling community or sexual orientation, or

[280] Section 7 of the Censorship of Films Act 1923

(iii) would tend, by reason of the inclusion in it of obscene or indecent matter, to deprave or corrupt persons who might view it, or

(iv) it depicts acts of gross violence or cruelty (including mutilation and torture) towards humans or animals[281].'

The Censorship of Publications Act 1946-1967 permits the censorship of publications which are 'indecent and obscene' or 'advocates the procurement of abortion or miscarriage[282].'

3. Respect for Authority of Courts and Due Process

Freedom of expression can be restricted in respect of prejudicial press reporting of proceedings pending or presently before the Courts.

- *Cullen v Toibin*[283]

O'Higgins CJ:

> '... [freedom of the press] can only be curtailed or restricted by the Courts in the manner sought in these proceedings where such action is necessary for the administration of justice.'

- *Kelly v O' Neill*[284]

Keane J:

> '... contempt of Court is committed... when a person publishes material which is calculated to interfere with

281 Section 3 of the Video Recordings Act 1989
282 Section 7 of the Censorship of Publications Act 1946
283 [1984] ILRM 577
284 [2000] 1 IR 354, [2000] 1 ILRM 507

> the course of justice: it is not a necessary ingredient of the offence that it results in such an interference.'

- *Irish Times Limited v Ireland*[285]

Hamilton CJ:

> '.... before a judge presiding over a trial imposes a ban on reporting he must be satisfied of two things: (a) that there is a real risk of an unfair trial, if contemporaneous reporting is permitted, and (b) that the damage which such improper reporting would cause could not be remedied by the trial judge either by appropriate directions to the jury or otherwise.'

- *Re Kennedy and McCann*[286]

Publication of in camera proceedings constitutes contempt of court.

4. Confidential Information

The right to freedom of expression can be restricted in respect of confidential information.

In *National Irish Bank v RTE*[287] the Supreme Court determined that, in certain circumstances, the public interest in defeating wrongdoing can outweigh the public interest in maintaining confidentiality.

5. Law of Defamation

Article 40.3.2 refers to the citizen's right to his/her good name and civil liability for defamatory statements is governed by the Defamation Act 2009.

---

[285] [1998] 1 IR 359, [1998] 2 ILRM 161
[286] [1976] IR 382
[287] [1998] 2 IR 465, [1998] 2 ILRM 196

The Courts will balance the citizen's right to his/her good name with the right to freedom of expression.

- *Hunter v Duckworth*[288]

O' Caoimh CJ:

> 'It is clear that in the context of Ireland being a democratic state, clear recognition has to be given to the right to freedom of expression. I believe that this right should not be undermined by the provisions of the Constitution relating to the protection of one's reputation. It is clear that the rights have to be construed on a harmonious basis. Nevertheless, it is clear that in certain cases, in the context of the democratic nature of the State, primacy may have to be given to freedom of expression.'

However, O' Caoimh J further determined that:

> 'One must proceed on the assumption that the courts in addressing individual cases will have regard to the circumstances of each case....'

- *Monica Leech v Independent Newspapers*[289]

Charleton J:

> '[T]here is a professional duty on the part of journalists to both seek out information that is of public interest [and that the Courts would consider whether] on the evidence the steps taken to gather and publish the information were responsible and fair [having regard to the] practical realities of news gathering.'

288 [2003] IEHC 81
289 [2007] IEHC 223

Note also: *Sinclair v Gogarty*[290], *Reynolds v Malocco*[291] and *Cogley v RTE*[292].

The courts will only grant an interlocutory injunction to prevent the publication of material in the clearest cases where there is no doubt but that the material is defamatory.

290 [1937] IR 377
291 [1999] 2 IR 203, [1999] 1 ILRM 289
292 [2005] 4 IR 79

13

Freedom of Association

Article 40.6.1. provides that:
'The State guarantees liberty for the exercise of the following rights, subject to public order and morality:

> "... (iii)The right of the citizens to form associations and unions."'

It further provides that:

> 'Laws, however, may be enacted for the regulation and control in the public interest of the exercise of the foregoing right.'

National Union of Railwaymen v Sullivan[293]

> 'The Constitution states the right of the citizens to form associations or unions in an emphatic way.'

Restrictions

Right of Freedom of Association is not absolute. It can be subject to restriction on the grounds of:

[293] [1947] IR 77, (1947) 81 ILTR 55

- Public order/state security: examples include certain provisions in Offences Against the State Act 1939, Offences Against the State (Amendment) Act 1972, Criminal Law Act 1976,
- Public morality: *Norris v AG*[294],
- Public interest.

National Union of Railwaymen v Sullivan[295]

Murnaghan J held that "...regulation and control in the public interest" must not eliminate the right of free association completely.

> 'Both logically and practically, to deprive a person of the choice of the persons with whom he will associate, is not a control of the exercise of the right of association, but a denial of the right altogether....it seems impossible to harmonise [Article 40.6.1iii] with a law which prohibits the forming of associations and unions, and allows the citizen only to join prescribed associations and unions... In the opinion of this Court, a law which takes away the right of the citizens, at their choice, to form associations and unions, not contrary to public order or morality, is not a law which can be validly made under the Constitution.'

- Restrictions on Membership

Equality Authority v Portmarnock Golf Club[296]

Hardiman J:

> 'There is a Constitutionally recognised right to freedom of association. At least in the private sphere one may associate with whom one likes and need not associate with

294 [1984] IR 36
295 [1947] IR 77, (1947) 81 ILTR 55
296 [2009] IESC 73

> those with whom one does not wish to associate. Thus, one may have a ladies' club, a gentlemens' club, a gay club, a Catholic club, an Africans' club and so on. And if one forms such a body, one may exclude from it those who do not meet the basic criterion for membership. Thus, a man may be excluded from a ladies' club and so on. This is the immemorial position at law, and is also agreed by all parties.'

In *Tierney v Amalgamated Society of Woodworkers*[297] it was held that trade unions and private associations have a right to accept and reject members.

Trade Union Membership

- *Murphy v Stewart*[298]

Article 40.6.1iii guarantees a right to form a trade union but not to join one.

- *Becton Dickinson v Lee*[299]

Membership of a particular union could be made a condition of employment.

- *Rodgers v ITGWU*[300]

A member of a trade union has a right to participate in the democratic and decision making processes of the Union subject to the rules of the union.

- *Doyle v Croke*[301]

---

297 [1959] IR 254
298 [1973] IR 97
299 [1973] IR 1
300 [1978] ILRM 51
301 12 May 1989, unreported, High Court

The right to freedom of association includes a right to fair procedures.

- *Dublin Colleges ASA v City of Dublin VEC*[302], *Association of General Practitioners v Minister for Health*[303], *Abbott and Whelan ITGWU*[304]

There is no obligation on an employer to enter into negotiations with a Union.

Freedom to Dissociate

Article 40.6.1iii creates an implied right to dissociate or not become a member.

Education Company of Ireland Ltd v Fitzpatrick (No. 2)[305]
Budd J:

> 'Taking the language of the Article quoted in its ordinary meaning it will be noted that what the State guarantees is liberty for the exercise of the right of the citizens to form associations and unions…I would myself construe the words of the Article as meaning by implication that a citizen has the correlative right not to form or join associations or unions if he does not wish to do so, and it seems to me to follow that in the case of associations or unions already formed he is free to associate or not as he pleases.'

Kingsmill Moore J found that the right of free dissociation arose by implication in Article 40.6.1iii:

302 31 July 1981, unreported, High Court
303 [1995] 1 IR 382, [1995] 2 ILRM 481
304 (1982) 1 JISLL 56
305 [1961] IR 345

> 'I think a guarantee of a right to form associations and unions is only intelligible where there is an implicit right to abstain from joining such associations or unions or, to put it another way, to associate and unite with those who do not join such unions.'

In *Meskellv CIE*[306] Walsh J in the Supreme Court affirmed that there was an implied right to dissociate.

306 [1973] IR 121

14

Right to Liberty – Article 40.4.1

Article 40.4.1 of the Constitution provides that 'No citizen shall be deprived of his personal liberty save in accordance with law.'

'In accordance with law'

Re Article 26 and the Offences against the State (Amendment) Bill 1940[307]

Sullivan CJ:

> '[It means] in accordance with the law as it exists at the time when the particular Article is invoked and sought to be applied…[A restriction on liberty must be] in accordance with the provisions of a statute duly passed by the Oireachtas; subject always to the qualification that such provisions are not repugnant to the Constitution or to any provision thereof.'

A person's liberty is restricted when detained following arrest and when imprisoned following conviction.

---

307 [1940] IR 470, (1940) 74 ILTR 61

Legislation which provides for a restriction of liberty will be assessed in accordance with the provisions of the Constitution.

King v Attorney General[308]
Henchy J:

> 'No citizen shall be deprived of personal liberty save in accordance with law - which means without stooping to methods which ignore the fundamental norms of the legal order postulated by the Constitution.'

Unlawful Detention and Imprisonment

Detainee

An accused can be arrested by warrant for an indictable offence or without a warrant pursuant to s 4 of Criminal Law Act 1997 if suspected, with reasonable cause, to be in the act of committing an arrestable offence or to have committed such an offence. Detention following arrest must be for the appropriate detention period permitted under statute and the conditions of detention must be in accordance with, *inter alia*, the Garda Custody Regulations 1987.

People (DPP) v Quilligan (No. 3)[309]

> '1. Where the arresting garda does not have a *bona fide* suspicion, the arrest is unlawful and the person may be released by an order pursuant to Article 40 of the Constitution;

[308] [1981] IR 233
[309] [1993] 2 IR 305

2. At the time of the arrest the suspect must be informed, if he does not already know, of the offence of which he is suspected, otherwise the arrest will be unlawful;
3. During his detention, the person has the right to legal assistance, and the refusal to grant a reasonable request for such assistance may make the detention unlawful;
4. The person detained has the right to medical assistance;
5. The person detained has the right of access to the courts;
6. The person detained has the right to remain silent and the associated right to be told of that right;
7. The Judges' Rules apply to a detention;
8. The person detained must not be subjected to unfair or oppressive questioning;
9. Where the detention is extended…the officer must *bona fide* entertain the suspicion that justified the original detention and must be satisfied that the further detention is necessary.'

However a detention will only be deemed unlawful where there has been 'a default of fundamental requirements that the detention may be said to be wanting in due process of law.'It is not enough to show that 'some defect or illegality attaches to his detention': per O' Higgins CJ in *The State (McDonagh) v Frawley*[310].

Challenge to Restrictions on the Liberty of a Prisoner and Hebeas Corpus

- *The State (Cannon) v Kavanagh*[311]

[310] [1978] IR 131
[311] [1937] IR 428, (1937) 71 ILTR 249

Maguire P:

> '...[a party who is detained following conviction and sentence is] *prima facia* detained according to law, and it would require most exceptional circumstances for this court to grant even a conditional order of habeas corpus to a prisoner so convicted.'

- *The State (Royal) v Kelly*[312]

Henchy J:

> 'It would be necessary to show that the procedure has been so flawed by basic defect as to make the conviction a nullity.'

- *The State (Aherne) v Cotter*[313]

> 'It has to be shown that the detention 'derives from a departure from the fundamental principles of natural justice.'

- *Gilligan v Governor of Portlaois Prison*[314]

McKechnie J:

> '[t]here is no iron curtain between the Constitution and the prisons in the Republic...a person convicted of an offence must understand that his loss of personal liberty, legally provided for, inevitably attaches to it, the abolition, albeit temporary, of some rights and the curtailment or restriction of others.'

- *Murray v Attorney General*[315]

312 [1974] IR 269
313 [1982] IR 188, [1983] ILRM 17
314 12 April 2001, unreported, High Court
315 [1985] IR 532, [1985] ILRM 542

Costello J:

> 'Those rights which may be exercised by a prisoner are those (a) which do not depend on the continuance of his personal liberty (so a prisoner cannot exercise his Constitutional right to earn a livelihood) or (b) which are compatible with the reasonable requirements of the place in which he is imprisoned, or to put it another way, do not impose unreasonable demands on it.'

However a serious breach of constitutional rights may entitle a prisoner to habeas corpus under Article 40.4.2.

- *The State (Richardson) v Governor of Mountjoy Prison*[316]

Barrington J:

> 'If a Court were convinced that the authorities were taking advantage of the fact the person was detained consciously and deliberately to violate his constitutional rights or to subject him to inhuman or degrading treatment, the Court might order his release. Likewise, if the Court were convinced that the conditions of a prisoner's detention were such as seriously to endanger his life or health, and that the authorities intended to do nothing to rectify these conditions, the Court might release him. It appears to me that the position would be similar if the conditions of a prisoner's detention were such as seriously to threaten his life or health, but the authorities were, for some reason, unable to rectify the conditions.'

[316] [1980] ILRM 82

15

Inviolability of Dwelling

Article 40.5

Article 40.5 of the Constitution provides that:

> 'The dwelling of every citizen is inviolable and shall not be forcibly entered save in accordance with law.'

Inviolability and Forcible Entry

- *People (AG) v Hogan*[317]

Kenny J:

> 'The dwelling of every citizen is inviolable and shall not be forcibly entered save in accordance with law. The guarantee is not against forcible entry only. The meaning of the Article is that the dwelling of every citizen is inviolable except to the extent that entry is permitted by law which may permit forcible entry.'

- *The People (Attorney General) v O' Brien*[318]

---

[317] (1972)1 Frewen 360

[318] [1965] IR 142

Walsh J:

> '[Article 40.5] does not mean that the guarantee is against forcible entry only. In my view, the reference to forcible entry is an intimation that forcible entry may be permitted by law but that in any event the dwelling of every citizen is inviolable save where entry is permitted by law and that, if necessary, such law may permit forcible entry.'

Meaning of Dwelling

- *The People (Attorney General) v O' Brien*[319]

Walsh J:

> 'If a member of a family occupies a clearly defined portion of the house apart from the other members of the family, then it may well be that the part not so occupied is no longer his dwelling and that the part he separately occupies is his dwelling as would be the case where a person not a member of the family occupied or was in possession of a clearly defined portion of the house.'

- *The People (DPP) v Lawless*[320]

Article 40.5 can only be pleaded by a party who is the owner or occupier of a dwelling.

The following do not constitute dwellings for the purpose of Article 40.5:

- The commercial portion of a mixed commercial/residential premises: *DPP v MacMahon*[321].

---

319 [1965] IR 142
320 (1984) 3 Frewen 30
321 [1986] IR 393

- The garden or driveway of a premises: *DPP v Corrigan*[322].

In Accordance with Law'

King v Attorney General[323]

Henchy J:

> '… [it means] without stooping to methods which ignore the fundamental norms of the legal order postulated by the Constitution.

Forcible entry of dwelling – is permitted at law in the following circumstances:

1. Common Law

The Gardai can enter a dwelling on foot of a search warrant issued by a District Court Judge or Peace Commissioner where the Gardai believe that stolen goods are on the property.

2. Under Statute

Certain statutory provisions allow entry onto a dwelling including:

- S 6 of the Criminal Law Act 1997

Power to enter and search a premises to effect an arrest on foot of a warrant (S 6(1)) or without a search warrant (S 6(2))

---

322 [1986] IR 290

323 [1981] IR 233

- Section 10 Criminal Justice (Miscellaneous Provisions) Act, 1997, as amended by s 6 of the 2006 Criminal Justice Act:

Power of search and seizure on foot of a warrant

- Section 7 of Child Trafficking and Pornography Act 1998, s 14 of the Criminal Assets Bureau Act 1996, s 8 of the Criminal Justice (Drug trafficking) Act 1996 which amended s 26 of the Misuse of Drugs Act 1977

These give powers of entry, search and seizure on the issuance of a warrant.

Byrne v Grey[324]

> '...[when issuing a warrant the] District Justice or Peace Commissioner should himself be satisfied by information on oath that facts exist which constitute reasonable grounds for suspecting that an offence has been or is being committed.'

Henchy J cited the decision of Lord Diplock in *R v IRC, ex parte Rossminister Ltd*[325] in finding that legislation which permits entry and search of a dwelling must be construed in a manner which is least restrictive to the Constitutional rights of an accused.

DPP v Dunne[326]

Carney J:

> 'The Constitutional protection given in Article 40, s 5 of the Constitution in relation to the inviolability of the

[324] [1988] IR 31
[325] [1980] AC 952
[326] [1994] 2 IR 537

> dwelling house is one of the most important, clear and unqualified protections given by the Constitution to the citizen.'

In this regard Carney J stated that a warrant must be in 'clear, complete, accurate and unambiguous terms'.

3. To Safeguard Constitutional Rights

DPP v Delaney[327]

O' Flaherty J:

> 'The sergeant was entitled to enter the premises to safeguard the life and limbs of a woman who was there as well as the children...He was entitled to make the choice that he did and such choice, far from being a breach of the Constitution, was in fulfilment of the obligation that devolves on all citizens to observe and implement the requirements of the Constitution because the safeguarding of life and limb must be more important than the inviolability of the dwelling of a citizen, especially when it is under attack in any event.'

4. Entry with Implied Consent

An owner/occupier can impliedly consent to entry onto a dwelling.

DPP v Forbes[328]

O' Flaherty J:

> 'It must be regarded as axiomatic that any householder gives an implied authority to a member of the garda

[327] [1997] 3 IR 453, [1998] 1 ILRM 507
[328] [1994] 2 IR 542, [1993] ILRM 817

> to come onto the forecourt of his premises to see to the enforcement of the law or prevent a breach thereof.'

Note also: *DPP v Gaffney*[329].

[329] [1987] IR 173, [1988] ILRM 39

16

Property Rights

Article 43 of the Constitution provides that:

> '1. 1° The State acknowledges that man, in virtue of his rational being, has the natural right, antecedent to positive law, to the private ownership of external goods.
>
> 2° The State accordingly guarantees to pass no law attempting to abolish the right of private ownership or the general right to transfer, bequeath, and inherit property.
>
> 2. 1° The State recognises, however, that the exercise of the rights mentioned in the foregoing provisions of this Article ought, in civil society, to be regulated by the principles of social justice.
>
> 2° The State, accordingly, may as occasion requires delimit by law the exercise of the said rights with a view to reconciling their exercise with the exigencies of the common good.'

In addition, Article 40.3.2 states that:

> 'The State shall, in particular, by its laws protect as best it may from unjust attack and, in the case of injustice done, vindicate the... property rights of every citizen.'

Article 43 and Article 40.3 can be invoked by human persons and corporate bodies: *Iarnrod Eireann v Ireland*[330].

Definition of Property

'Property' is widely defined and has been held to include land, ownership of land, rights arising from the ownership of land, chattels, moveable property, money, intangible rights, shares, licenses, the right to earn a livelihood and the right to litigate.

Relationship between Article 43 and Article 40.3

Blake v Attorney General[331]

O' Higgins CJ:

> '[Article 43] prohibits the abolition of private property as an institution, but at the same time permits, in particular circumstances, the regulation of the exercise of that right and of the general right to transfer, bequeath and inherit property.'
>
> '[Article 40.3] deals with the citizen's right to a particular item of property.'

However, the Courts now recognise a close connection between both Articles 43 and 40.3.2 of the Constitution. In determining whether there has been an unjust attack on the property rights of the citizen in Article 40.3.2 the Courts will have regard to the principles of social justice and the exigencies of the common good specified in Article 43.2.1 and vice versa.

330 [1996] 2 IR 321
331 [1982] IR 117

Note: *Dreher v Irish Land Commission*[332], *Caffola v O'Malley*[333], *O'Callaghan v Commissioner of Public Works*[334], *ESB v Gormley*[335], *Madigan v Attorney General*[336], *Pine Valley Developments Ltd v Minister for the Environment*[337], *Re Article 26 and the Employment Equality Bill*[338], *Re Article 26* and *Part V of the Planning and Development Bill 1999*[339].

Restrictions

The property rights of the citizen are not absolute. They can be subject to restriction provided that any such restriction does not constitute an unjust attack.

A restriction will not constitute an unjust attack where:

(a) the objective for such restriction can be justified by principles of social justice and the exigencies of the common good;

(b) the measures for securing that objective are compatible with the constitution;

(c) the measures are proportionate to the objective sought to be achieved.

Shirley v O'Gorman[340]

Peart J:

332 [1984] ILRM 94
333 [1985] IR 486
334 [1985] ILRM 364
335 [1985] IR 129, [1985] ILRM 494
336 [1986] ILRM 136
337 [1987] IR 23
338 [1997] 2 IR 321, [1997] 8 ELR 132
339 [2000] 2 IR 321
340 [2012] IESC 5

'Until some point of absolute extremity is reached where legislation is patently and manifestly not in pursuit of any possible common good exigency, the Court should abstain from interfering with the role of the legislature in deciding what measures are needed.'

Restrictions Amounting to Unjust Attack

Case law	Measure constituting an unjust attack
Brennan v Attorney General[341]	Imposition of rates on landowners based on valuations over a century old
Buckley v Attorney General[342]	Introduction of legislation to determine ownership of monies and terminate proceedings on the issue of establishing ownership
Blake v Attorney General[343]	Restrictions on rent payable to landlords of controlled dwellings under the Rent Restrictions Act 1960
Re Article 26 and the Housing (Private Rented Dwelling) Bill 1981[344]	The phasing out of rent control over a five year period through the payment of rebates to landlords which were substantially less than the full open market value of rent

(*Continued*)

341 [1983] ILRM 449 (HC), [1984] ILRM 355 (SC)
342 [1950] IR 67
343 [1982] IR 117
344 [1983] IR 181

(*Continued*)

Cox v Ireland[345]	The requirement on State employees under s 34 of the Offences Against the State Act 1939 to forfeit any pension, superannuation, allowance or gratuity earned in respect of any service rendered prior to the date of conviction for a Scheduled Offence in the Special Criminal Court.
Re Article 26 and the Employment Equality Bill 1996[346]	The significant costs imposed on employers in the provision of facilities for disabled employees
Re Article 26 and the Health (Amendment)(No. 2) Bill 2004[347]	The prohibition on an action against the State to recover medical charges for inpatient services.

Restrictions not Amounting to Unjust Attack

The following measures have been held not to amount to unjust attack on the basis of the principles of social justice, the exigencies of the common good and the doctrine of proportionality:

345 [1992] 2 IR 503
346 [1997] 2 IR 321, [1997] 8 ELR 132
347 [2005] 1 IR 205

Case law	**Measure held not to constitute an unjust attack**
Gilligan v Criminal Assets Bureau & others[348], *Murphy v GM*[349]	Forfeiture of property which is proved, on the balance of probabilities, to represent the proceeds of crime under the Proceeds of Crime Act 1996
Article 26 and Part V of the Planning and Development Bill 1999[350]	The condition attached to the grant of planning that up to 20% of land zoned for residential or mixed residential and other uses would be ceded to local authorities at a price less than market value for the provision of social and affordable housing.
J & J Haire & Company Ltd v Minister for Health and Children[351]	Reduction in fees paid to pharmacists was justified 'in the interest of avoiding an extreme financial crisis or a fundamental disequilibrium in public finances.'
Caffola v O' Malley[352]	restrictions on the use of gaming machines
O' Callaghan v Commissioner of Public Works[353]	Restrictions on land use under the National Monuments Act 1930 for the protection of national monuments

(*Continued*)

348 [1998] 3 IR 185
349 [2001] 4 IR 113
350 [2000] 2 IR 321
351 [2009] IEHC 562
352 [1985] IR 486
353 [1985] ILRM 364

(*Continued*)

O' Brien v Bord Na Móna[354]	the compulsory acquisition of bogland to develop the country's peat resources
Madigan v Attorney General[355]	residential property tax on owner/ occupiers of residential property.
Clancy v Ireland[356]	freezing of money held in bank accounts operated on behalf of unlawful organisations under the Offences against the State Act 1985
Lawlor v Minister for Agriculture[357]	milk quotas/superlevy system on the production of milk
Hand v Dublin Corporation[358]	restrictions placed on the granting of casual trading licences
Iarnrod Eireann v Ireland[359]	Subsections 12 and 14 of the Civil Liability Act 1961 which provides for joint and several liability of joint tortfeasors
Liddy v Minister for Public Enterprise[360]	Restrictions on the right of landowners to obtain planning permission for development on lands adjacent to airports in the interest of flight safety.

(*Continued*)

354 [1983] IR 255, [1983] ILRM 314
355 [1986] ILRM 136
356 [1988] IR 326, [1989] ILRM 670
357 [1990] 1 IR 356
358 [1991] 1 IR 409
359 [1996] 2 IR 321
360 4 February 2003, unreported, High Court

(*Continued*)

Brady v Haughton[361]	retention by Gardaí of property seized as part of a lawful arrest for the purpose of a criminal prosecution
Hempenstall v Minister for Environment[362], *Gorman v Minister for Environment (No. 2)*[363]	Deregulation of taxi licenses leading to a reduction in the value of taxi licenses

Compensation for Acquisition

A compulsory acquisition of property will be unconstitutional where the party whose lands have been acquired has not been adequately compensated.

In addition, a compulsory acquisition must only be undertaken in the interests of the common good: *Clinton v An Bord Pleanala*[364], *Egan v An Bord Pleanála and Athlone Town Council*[365]

Central Dublin Development Association v Attorney General[366]

Kenny J:

> '[T]he acquisition by the State of all the rights which together make up ownership without compensation

[361] [2005] IESC 54
[362] [1994] 2 IR 20, [1993] ILRM 318
[363] [2001] 2 IR 414
[364] [2007] IESC 19
[365] [2011] IEHC 44
[366] (1975) 109 ILTR 69

would in almost all cases be [an unjust attack on the property rights of the citizen].'

Article 26 and Part V of the Planning and Development Bill 1999[367]

Keane CJ:

'There can be no doubt that a person who is compulsorily deprived of his or her property in the interests of the common good should normally be fully compensated at a level equivalent to at least the market value of the acquired property'.

Compensation may not be required where justifiable restrictions are placed on property rights: *Dreher v Irish Land Commission*[368].

However, in *Re Article 26* and *The Health (Amendment) (No. 2) Bill 2004*[369] Murray CJ held that "in practice, substantial encroachment on rights, without compensation, will rarely be justified."

[367] [2000] 2 IR 321
[368] [1984] ILRM 94
[369] [2005] 1 IR 205

17

The Family, The Child and Education

Article 41.1 of the Constitution refers to the family as 'the natural primary and fundamental unit group of Society' and 'a moral institution possessing inalienable and imprescriptible rights, antecedent and superior to all positive law.'

Article 41.2 provides that the State 'guarantees to protect the Family in its constitution and authority, as the necessary basis of social order and as indispensable to the welfare of the Nation and the State.'

Definition of the Family

The family for the purposes of the Constitution is one which is based on marriage between a man and a woman.

State (Nicolaou) v An Bord Uchtála[370]

Walsh J:

> 'It is quite clear from the provisions of Article 41, and in particular section 3 thereof, that the family referred

[370] [1966] IR 567, (1986) 102 ILTR 1

> to in this Article is the family which is founded on the institution of marriage and, in the context of the Article, marriage means valid marriage under the law for the time being in force in the State.'

Cohabiting and same sex couples are not considered a constitutional family and cannot rely on the provisions of Articles 41 and 42.

McD v L & Anor[371]

Denham J:

> 'There is no institution in Ireland of a *de facto* family.'

Marriage

Marriage under the Constitution is between parties of the opposite sex.

This is evident from the following decisions:

Murray v Ireland[372]

Costello J:

> '....the Constitution makes clear that the concept and nature of marriage, which it enshrines, are derived from the Christian notion of partnership based on an irrevocable personal consent, given by both spouses which establishes a unique and very special lifelong relationship.'

TF v Ireland[373]

371 [2007] IESC 81

372 [1985] IR 532, [1985] ILRM 542

373 [1995] 1 IR 321, [1994] 2 ILRM 321(Supreme Court)

McKechnie J:

> 'In this and in the neighbouring jurisdiction...it is crucial for legal purposes that the parties should be of the opposite biological sex.'

Foy v Registrar of Births Deaths and Marriages[374]
McKechnie J:

> 'It seems to me that marriage as understood by the Constitution, by statute and by case law refers to the union of a biological man with a biological woman.'

Zappone & Gilligan v Revenue Commissioners[375]
Dunne J:

> 'Marriage was understood under the 1937 Constitution to be confined to persons of the opposite sex...That has always been the definition...I accept that the Constitution is a living instrument...but I also accept...that there is a difference between an examination of the Constitution in the context of ascertaining unenumerated rights and redefining a right which is implicit in the Constitution and which is clearly understood. In this case the court is being asked to redefine marriage to mean something which it has never done to date.'

Safeguarding Marriage from Attack

Article 43.1 of the Constitution states that 'the State pledges itself to guard with special care the institution of Marriage, on which the Family is founded, and to protect it against attack.'

---

[374] [2002] IEHC 116
[375] [2006] IEHC 404

A legislative provision which undermines the institution of marriage can be deemed unconstitutional.

Murphy v Attorney General[376]

> '[The pledge to] guard with special care the institution of marriage is a guarantee that this institution in all its constitutional connotations ...will be given special protection so that it will continue to fulfill its function as the basis of the family and as a permanent, indissoluble union of man and woman.'

Note also: *Hyland v Minister for Social Welfare*[377], *Greene v Minister for Agriculture*[378], *Re Article 26* and the *Matrimonial Home Bill 1993*[379]

The constitutional protection of the institution of marriage may result in positive discrimination in favour of the marital family: *O'B v S*[380].

Mhic Mhathuna v Ireland[381]

Carroll J ruled that additional State support directed at single parents did not amount to an inducement not to marry thereby undermining the institution of marriage. Instead, such supports were "child centered and cannot... be designated as an attack on the institution of marriage."

---

376 [1982] IR 241
377 [1989] IR 624; [1990] ILRM 213
378 [1990] 2 IR 17, [1990] ILRM 364
379 [1994] 1 IR 305
380 [1984] IR 316, [1985] ILRM 86
381 [1989] IR 504

Children's Rights

In matters relating to the welfare of the child such as guardianship, custody, access and adoption, the best interests of the child must be the paramount consideration.
In *G v An Bord Uchtála*[382] Walsh J determined that the word 'paramount''certainly indicates that the welfare of the child is to be the superior or the most important consideration'.

The State however will only intervene in exceptional circumstances where there are compelling reasons justifying intervention.

North Western Health Board v HW[383]

Denham J:

> '...the family as a moral institution enjoys certain liberties under the Constitution which protects it from undue interference by the State whereas the State may intervene in exceptional circumstances in the interest of the common good or where the parents have failed for physical or moral reasons in their duty towards their children... Decisions which are sometimes taken by parents concerning their children may be a source of discomfort or even distress to the rational and objective bystander, but it seems to me that there must be something exceptional arising from a failure of duty...before the State can intervene in the interest of the individual child.'

Denham J concluded that:

> 'It would be impossible and undesirable to seek to define in one neat rule or formula all the circumstances in which

[382] [1980] IR 32, (1979) 113 ILTR 25
[383] [2001] 3 IR 622

the State might intervene in the interests of the child against the express wishes of the parent. It seems however to me that there must be some immediate and fundamental threat to the capacity of the child to continue to function as a human person, physically morally or socially, deriving from an exceptional dereliction of duty on the part of parents to justify such an intervention.'

McK v Information Commissioner[384]

In this case, it was held that there is a rebuttable presumption that a parent is entitled to access to the medical records of a child and that any such access is in the interest of the child. Denham J found that:

> 'A parent...has rights and duties in relation to a child. It is presumed that his or her actions are in accordance with the best interests of the child. This presumption while not absolute is fundamental.'

In addition there is a constitutional presumption that the interests of the child are served by placing the child with its constitutional family (natural married parents).

Re JH[385]

Finlay CJ:

> '[There is] a Constitutional presumption that the welfare of ....a child is to be found within the family unless the Court is satisfied that there are compelling reasons why this cannot be achieved or the evidence establishes an exceptional case where the parents have, for moral or physical reasons, failed, and continue to fail to provide education for the child.'

---

384 [2006] 1 IR 260

385 [1985] IR 375, [1985] ILRM 302

N & N v Health Service Executive (Baby Ann Case)[386]

In this case, the Supreme Court endorsed the 'compelling reasons' test developed in *Re JH* and, in awarding custody to the natural parents, McGuinness J found that on the marriage of the natural parents they 'became a constitutional family with all the concomitant rights and presumptions.'

McGuinness J stated that the "constitutional presumption that the welfare of the child is to be found within the family" applies "to the legally married family alone."

Article 42A

provides *inter alia*, that:

- The State recognises and affirms the natural and imprescriptible rights of all children and shall, as far as practicable, by its laws protect and vindicate those rights.
- In exceptional cases, where the parents, regardless of their marital status, fail in their duty towards their children to such extent that the safety or welfare of any of their children is likely to be prejudicially affected, the State as guardian of the common good shall, by proportionate means as provided by law, endeavour to supply the place of the parents, but always with due regard for the natural and imprescriptible rights of the child[387].

[386] [2006] IESC 60

[387] The result of the referendum inserting Article 42A is under appeal to the Supreme Court in In the Matter of the Referendum on the Proposal for the Amendment of the Constitution contained in the

Rights of Family are not Absolute

Murray v Ireland[388]

Costello J:

> 'No reference is made in Article 41 to any restrictive power, but it is clear that the exercise by the Family of its imprescriptible and inalienable right to integrity as a unit group can be severely and validly restricted by the State...'

However in *Article 26* and the *Matrimonial Home Bill 1993*[389] Finlay CJ held that any interference with the rights of the family must be reasonable and proportionate and must go no more than necessary to secure legitimate aims.

Fajujonu v Minister for Justice[390]

A non-Irish Citizen can be refused entry into the jurisdiction or deported even if he/she is married to an Irish citizen or is a parent of an Irish citizen.

Finlay J held that the reason to justify removal of a family from the State must be "... a grave and substantial reason associated with the common good".

Finlay J determined however that:

> '...there can be no question but that those children, as citizens, have a constitutional right to the company, care and parentage of their [non-citizen] parents within a family unit. I am also satisfied that *prima facie* and subject to the exigencies of the common good that that is a right which

---

Thirty First Amendment of the Constitution (Children) Bill 2012, held on 10 November 2012 [2013] IEHC 458

388 [1985] IR 532, [1985] ILRM 542

389 [1994] 1 IR 305

390 [1990] 2 IR 151

> these citizens should be entitled to exercise within the State.'

See also: *Osheku v Ireland*[391], *Abdelkefi v Ireland*[392], *Pok Sun Shum v Ireland*[393]

Lobe & Osayande v The Minister for Justice[394]

Fennelly J. in the Supreme Court held that the Minister could deport the non-national parents of an Irish citizen in "exceptional circumstances associated with the common good" even if this were to result in the "*de facto* deportation of the child".

Cirpaci v Minister for Justice[395]

Fennelly J ruled that, in considering the right of residence of a non-citizen who has married an Irish Citizen:

> 'It is legitimate for the Minister to have regard to the duration of the marriage relationship when weighing in the balance the family rights in question.'

Dimbo & Oguekwe v Minister for Justice[396]

In this case, Denham J held that, in making a decision whether to deport a non-citizen parent of an Irish child, the Minister must have regard to

> '... the Constitutional and Convention rights of the applicant. This includes express consideration of, and a reasoned decision on, the rights of the Irish Citizen child.'

---

391 [1986] IR 733, [1987] ILRM 330
392 [1984] ILRM 138
393 [1986] ILRM 593
394 [2003] 1 IR 1
395 [2005] IESC 42
396 [2008] IESC 26, [2008] IESC 25

Education

Ryan v Attorney General[397]

O' Dalaigh CJ defined education as:

> '... the teaching and training of a child to make the best possible use of his inherent and potential capacities, physical, mental and moral.'

Article 42.1

recognises the family as:

> '... the primary and natural educator of the child [and provides that the State] guarantees to respect the inalienable right and duty of parents to provide, according to their means, for the religious and moral, intellectual, physical and social education of their children.'

Article 42.2

states that parents are:

> '... free to provide this education in their homes or in private schools or in schools recognised or established by the State.'

Article 42.3

provides that parents cannot be obliged:

> '... to send their children to schools established by the State, or to any particular type of school designated by the State.'

---

[397] [1965] IR 294

In *O' Shiel v Minister for Education*[398] Laffoy J recognised that "in its entirety, [Article 42] is imbued with the concept of parental freedom of choice."

Article 42.3.2

> 'The State shall, however, as guardian of the common good, require in view of actual conditions that the children receive a certain minimum education, moral, intellectual and social.'

DPP v Best[399]

Denham J considered the definition of 'a certain minimum education':

> 'This is a minimum standard of elementary education of a general character but should have regard to the intellectual and other capacities of the child. It is not necessarily equivalent to the primary school curriculum. It is a minimum education moral, intellectual and social which must be considered in light of factors including those previously reviewed such as the time the issue is determined, the family, the parents, their means, the child, the geographical situation, the actual circumstances and the common good. In balancing these factors which is not an exhaustive list the District Judge should while recognising the parental and family rights at the same time acknowledge the child's constitutional rights and the duty of the State as guardian of the common good. An education which creates a discriminatory situation for the child may establish circumstances where the rights of the child and the interest of the common good outweigh considerations of the family and parental rights.'

[398] [1999] 2 ILRM 241

[399] [1998] 2 ILRM 549

The State will accordingly intervene where a child is not receiving a suitable minimum standard of education.

Article 42.4

Imposes an obligation on the State to provide free primary education.

Crowley v Ireland[400]

Kenny J:

> '… the State is under no obligation to educate… the State is to provide the buildings, to pay to the teachers who are under no contractual duty to it but to the manager or trustees, to provide means of transport to the school if this is necessary to avoid hardship, and to prescribe minimum standards.'

Kenny J held that the duty on the State was to provide the means of education and it was the duty of the board of management to ensure that the education was provided.

The duty on the State to provide free primary education extends to providing for the needs of children with learning difficulties and special needs.

O' Donoghue v Minister for Health[401]

O' Hanlon J:

> '[T]here is a constitutional obligation imposed on the State by the provisions of Article 42.4 of the Constitution to provide for free basic elementary education of all children and that this involves giving each child such advice,

---

400 [1980] IR 102

401 [1996] 2 IR 20

instruction and teaching as will enable him or her to make the best possible use of his or her inherent and potential capacities, physical, mental and moral, however limited these capacities may be.'

Comerford v Minister for Education[402]
McGuinness J:

'[T]he right to free primary education extends to every child, although the education provided must vary in accordance with the child's abilities and needs.'

Sinnott v Minister for Education[403]
Murray J:

'[T]he State has an obligation to ensure that [primary education] is provided free to children who can benefit from it including those who suffer from severe mental or physical handicap.'

However the Supreme Court found that, adopting the historical method of Constitutional interpretation to consider the meaning of the word *'leanaí'*, the obligation on the State to provide free primary education ceases at the age of 18.

In *O' Carolan v Minister for Education*[404] MacMenamin J held that the education provided must be appropriate to the needs of the child.

402 [1997] 2 ILRM 134
403 [2001] 2 IR 545
404 [2005] IEHC 296

18

Religion

Article 44

'1. The State acknowledges that the homage of public worship is due to Almighty God. It shall hold His Name in reverence, and shall respect and honour religion.

2. 1° Freedom of conscience and the free profession and practice of religion are, subject to public order and morality, guaranteed to every citizen.'

In *Corway v Independent Newspapers*[405] Barrington J referred to Article 44.1 as placing a " duty on the State to respect and honour religion".

McGee v Attorney General[406]

Walsh J held that Article 44.2.1 guarantees:

'[T]he right not to be compelled or coerced into living in a way which is contrary to ones conscience and in the context of the Article that means contrary to one's conscience so far as the exercise practice or profession of religion is concerned.'

---

405 [1999] 4 IR 484

406 [1974] IR 284, (1975) 109 ILTR 29

Limitations on the Right

The right to freedom religion is not absolute. It is subject to limitations on the grounds of public order and morality.

Murphy v Independent Radio and Television Commission[407]

Barrington J held that the ban on religious advertising, introduced:

> '... to prevent the resentment and unrest from the broadcasting of advertisements on matters that had proved divisive in the past [and] to prevent the rich buying access to the airwaves [was] justified on proportionality grounds.'

Quinn's Supermarket Ltd v Attorney General[408]

Walsh J, in holding that provision should be made in regulating trading hours for the fact that the Jewish Sabbath fell on a Saturday, held that

> 'It would be completely contrary to the spirit and intendment of the provisions of Article 44, s 2, to permit the guarantee against discrimination on the ground of religious profession or belief to be made the very means of restricting or preventing the free profession or practice of religion'

Temple Street Hospital v D[409]

Hogan J:

> 'Given that Article 40.3.2 commits the State to protecting by its laws as best it may the life and person of every citizen, it is incontestable but that this Court is given a jurisdiction (and, indeed, a duty) to override the religious

[407] [1998] 2 ILRM 360
[408] [1972] IR 1
[409] [2011] IEHC 1

> objections of the parents where adherence to these beliefs would threaten the life and general welfare of their child.'

State not to Endow any Religion

Article 44.2.2°:

'The State guarantees not to endow any religion.'

The State is prohibited from promoting any one religion.

In *Campaign to Separate Church and State v Minister for Education*[410] Keane J adopted the definition of 'endow' in the Oxford English Dictionary 'to enrich with property; to provide (by bequest or gift) a *permanent* income for a person, society or institution.'

However the Supreme Court determined that Article 44.2.2 does not prohibit the State from providing monies to denominational schools.

Keane J determined that:

> '[Article 44.2.4°] makes it clear beyond argument... that the State is entitled to provide aid to schools under the management of different religious denominations.'

Note also: *McGrath and O' Ruairc v Trustees of Maynooth College*[411], *Re Article 26* and the *Employment Equality Bill 1996*[412].

The prohibition on the endowment of religion and religious discrimination applies only to the State and not to private parties, even where such parties receive

[410] [1998] 3 IR 321, [1998] 2 ILRM 81
[411] [1979] ILRM 166
[412] [1997] 2 IR 321, [1997] 8 ELR 132

funding from the State: *McGrath and O' Ruairc v Trustees of Maynooth College*[413].

No Discrimination on Religious Grounds

Article 44.2.3°:

> 'The State shall not impose any disabilities or make any discrimination on the ground of religious profession, belief or status.'

McGrath and O' Ruairc v Trustees of Maynooth College[414]
Henchy J:

> 'The constitutional provision invoked [in Article 44.2.3°] must be construed in terms of its purpose. In proscribing disabilities and discriminations at the hands of the State on the grounds of religious profession, belief or status, the primary aim of the constitutional guarantee is to give vitality, independence and freedom to religion.'

Quinn's Supermarket v Attorney General[415]
Walsh J referred to the word 'disabilities' and stated that:

> '...where the provision speaks of disabilities, the disability must be one which is suffered and imposed on the ground of the religious profession, belief or status of the person so disabled.'

In relation to the term 'discrimination' Walsh J commented that:

---

413 [1979] ILRM 166
414 [1979] ILRM 166
415 [1972] IR 1

'To discriminate, in that sense, is to create a difference between persons or bodies or to distinguish between them on the ground of religious profession, belief or status; it follows, therefore, that the religious profession, belief or status does not have to be that of the person who feels he has suffered by reason of the distinction created.'

Walsh J found however that a provision which created a distinction on the grounds of religious belief would not be unconstitutional where its purpose was to permit the free practice of religion:

'Any law which by virtue of the generality of its application would by its effect restrict or prevent the free profession and practice of religion...would be invalid having regard to the provisions of the Constitution, unless it contained provisions which saved from such restriction or prevention the practice of religion of the person or persons who would otherwise be so restricted or prevented.'

State Aid for Schools

Article 44.2.4°

'Legislation providing State aid for schools shall not discriminate between schools under the management of different religious denominations, nor be such as to affect prejudicially the right of any child to attend a school receiving public money without attending religious instruction at that school.'

Campaign to Separate Church and State v Minister for Education[416]

---

[416] [1998] 3 IR 321, [1998] 2 ILRM 81

Keane J:

'[Article 44.2.4°] makes it clear beyond argument, not merely that the State is entitled to provide aid to schools under the management of different religious denominations, but that such schools may also include religious instruction as a subject in their curricula. It is subject to two qualifications; first, the legislation must not discriminate between schools under the management of different religious denominations and, secondly, it must respect the right of a child not to attend religious instruction in a school in receipt of public funds.'

Barrington J noted however that:

'The Constitution therefore distinguishes between religious 'education' and religious 'instruction' - the former being the much wider term. A child who attends a school run by a religious denomination different from his own may have a Constitutional right not to attend religious instruction at that school but the Constitution cannot protect him from being influenced, to some degree, by the religious 'ethos' of the school. A religious denomination is not obliged to change the general atmosphere of its school merely to accommodate a child of a different religious persuasion who wishes to attend that school.'

Autonomy of Religious Denominations

Article 44.2.5°:

'Every religious denomination shall have the right to manage its own affairs, own, acquire and administer property, movable and immovable, and maintain institutions for religious or charitable purposes.'

This is a recognition of autonomous denominational rights.

McGrath & O' Rourke v Trustees of the College of Maynooth[417]
Henchy J:

> 'Far from eschewing the internal disabilities and discriminations which flow from the tenets of a particular religion the State must on occasion recognise and buttress them... they are part of the texture and essence of the particular religion; so, the State, in order to comply with the spirit and purpose inherent in this constitutional guarantee, may justifiably lend its weight to what may be thought to be disabilities and discriminations deriving from within a particular religion.'

Re Article 26 and the Employment Equality Bill 1996[418]
Hamilton CJ:

> '...it was Constitutionally permissible to make distinctions or discriminations on grounds of religious profession belief or status, insofar, but only insofar as this may be necessary to give life and reality to the guarantee of free profession and practice of religion contained in the Constitution.'

In *McNally v Ireland*[419] McMenamin J cited with approval the aforementioned judgments of Henchy and Hamilton JJ and found that:

> '...this may be seen as an 'occasion' where the State may recognise and buttress the tenets of a particular religion, insofar as it does not in any way impinge on the beliefs

[417] [1979] ILRM 166
[418] [1997] 2 IR 321
[419] [2009] IEHC 573

of other denominations or citizens. The State may thus justifiably even lend its weight to what might possibly be portrayed as a discrimination of status deriving from within Roman Catholicism. But such limited support (if there be such) does not constitute any prejudicial State intrusion or 'discrimination' where the status of a priest or in organised religion is advanced justifiably over a lay person or a business.'

19

Right to Life of Unborn

Article 40.3.3

'The State acknowledges the right to life of the unborn and, with due regard to the equal right to life of the mother, guarantees in its laws to respect, and, as far as practicable, by its laws to defend and vindicate that right.

This subsection shall not limit freedom to travel between the State and another state.

This subsection shall not limit freedom to obtain or make available, in the State, subject to such conditions as may be laid down by law, information relating to services lawfully available in another state.'

Transition of the Law on the Right to Life and Termination by Abortion

Recognition as an Unenumerated Right

McGee v The Attorney General[420]

---

[420] [1974] IR 284

In this case, Walsh J, while recognising the right to marital privacy, also referred to the right to life of the unborn child in the following terms:

> '[A]ny action on the part of either the husband and wife or of the State to limit family sizes by endangering or destroying human life must necessarily not only be an offence against the common good but also against the guaranteed personal rights of the human life in question.'

However, the decision of the United States Supreme Court in *Roe v Wade*[421] recognised that the right to privacy encompassed a right to have an abortion.

8th Amendment to Constitution

In 1983, as a result of the 8th Amendment to the Constitution, Article 40.3.3° was inserted into Bunreachtna h-Éireann providing that:

> 'The State acknowledges the right to life of the unborn and, with due regard to the equal right to life of the mother, guarantees in its laws to respect, and as far as practicable, by its laws to defend and vindicate that right.'

Cases on the Distribution of Information on Abortion

- *The Attorney General (SPUC) v Open Door Counselling Ltd*[422]

In this case, relating to the distribution of information on abortion services available in the United Kingdom, Finlay CJ ruled that:

---

421 410 US 113 1973

422 [1988] IR 593

> '...there could not be an implied and unenumerated constitutional right to information about the availability of a service of abortion outside the State which, if availed of, would have the direct consequence of destroying the expressly guaranteed Constitutional right to life of the unborn.'

This decision was reaffirmed by the Supreme Court in *SPUC V Grogan*[423].

- ***Attorney General v X* and Constitutional Amendment**

In the landmark decision of the Supreme Court in the *X Case*[424] Finlay CJ found that:

> '[I]f it is established as a matter of probability that there is a real and substantial risk to the life, as distinct from the health, of the mother, which can only be avoided by the termination of her pregnancy, such termination is permissible...'

It was ruled that suicide constitutes a real and substantial risk to the life of the mother.

Following the 13th and 14th Amendments to the Irish Constitution in the aftermath of the X Case, Article 40.3.3° as it is presently constituted was inserted into the Constitution.

The provision of information on abortion services being provided in other jurisdictions is governed by the Regulation of Information (Services outside the State for Termination of Pregnancies) Act 1995 (the Abortion Information Act).

---

[423] [1989] IR 753

[424] [1992] 1 IR 1, [1992] ILRM 401, [1992] 2 CMLR 277

Other Noteworthy Developments

- *MR v TR*[425]

The Supreme Court ruled that Article 40.3.3 protection does not cover frozen embryos. Denham J espoused that:

> 'The words of Article 40.3.3 refers to a situation where the rights of the mother and the unborn are engaged. This occurs after plantation. Thus Article 40.3.3 does not apply to pre-implantation embryos.'

Note also: *A and B v The Eastern Health Board, Judge Mary Fahy and C and The Attorney General*[426], *D v Health Service Executive*[427]

- in *A, B and C v Ireland*[428]

The European Court of Human Rights held that the failure of the Irish State to implement legislation governing the constitutional right to have an abortion where there was a risk to the life of the mother constituted a violation of Article 8 of the European Convention on Human Rights.

- Protection of Life in Pregnancy Act 2013

It is lawful to terminate a pregnancy under this Act where:

1. Two medical practitioners certify that there is a real and substantial risk of loss of the woman's life from a physical illness and that risk, in their reasonable

[425] [2006] IEHC 359
[426] [1998] 1 ILRM 460
[427] 9 May 2007, unreported, High Court
[428] [2010] ECHR 2032

opinion can only be averted by carrying out the medical procedure[429];

2. A medical practitioner certifies that there is an immediate risk of loss of the woman's life from a physical illness and the medical procedure is, in his or her reasonable opinion, immediately necessary in order to save the life of the woman[430];
3. Three medical practitioners certify that there is a real and substantial risk of loss of the woman's life by way of suicide and, in their reasonable opinion, that risk can only be averted by carrying out the medical procedure[431].

---

429 S 7

430 S8

431 S9

20

Trial in Due Course of Law

Article 38.1:

> 'No person shall be tried on any criminal charge save in due course of law.'

State (Healy) v Donoghue[432]

O' Higgins CJ:

> "[D]ue course of law' meant the procedures applied shall be fair and that the person accused shall be afforded every opportunity to defend himself.'

Presumption of Innocence

The right to due process in Article 38.1 includes the presumption of innocence, under which an accused is presumed innocent until his/her guilt is established by the prosecution.

Hardy v Ireland[433]

Hederman J:

---

432 [1976] IR 325

433 [1994] 2 IR 550

'[T]he Constitutional requirement of trial in due course of law protects the presumption of innocence; it requires that the prosecution should prove its case beyond all reasonable doubt; but it does not prohibit that, in the course of the case, once certain facts are established, inference may not be drawn from those facts....'

The burden of proof is on the prosecution to prove the guilt of the accused beyond all reasonable doubt.

Woolmington v DPP[434]

Viscount Sankey LC:

'Throughout the web of the English criminal law one golden thread is always to be seen, that it is the duty of the prosecution to prove the prisoner's guilt subject to ... the defence of insanity and subject also to any statutory exception.'

O' Leary v AG[435]

This case determined that legislation will not be a breach of Article 38.1 where it provides that certain conduct is evidence of (but not proof of) guilt and the evidential burden of proof shifts to the accused to challenge the veracity of any such evidence.

Costello J:

'... if the effect of the statute is that the Court must convict an accused should he or she fail to adduce exculpatory evidence then its effect is to shift the legal burden of proof.... whereas if its effect is that notwithstanding its terms the accused may be acquitted even though he calls no evidence because the statute has not discharged the

434 [1935] AC 462
435 [1995] 1 IR 454

prosecution from establishing the accused's guilt beyond a reasonable doubt then no Constitutional invalidity could arise'.

Right to Silence/Privilege against Self Incrimination

Article 38.1 includes a right to remain silent.

The right to silence however is not absolute and in *Heaney v Ireland*[436] Flaherty J applied the following proportionately test:

> 'The State is entitled to encroach on the right of the citizen to remain silent in pursuit of its entitlement to maintain public order and peace... In this pursuit the Constitutional rights of the citizen must be affected as little as possible.'

- *Rock v Ireland*[437]

Hamilton CJ:

> 'There is no doubt that the right to silence and the presumption of innocence in a criminal trial are implicit in the terms of the Constitution...[However], the right to silence is not absolute but is subject to public order and morality.'

Adverse inferences must not be drawn from the silence of an accused.

- *People (DPP) v Finnerty*[438]

In this case, Keane J considered an accused's failure to answer questions in the Garda Station and held that the right to silence:

---

436 [1996] 1 IR 580
437 [1998] 2 ILRM 38
438 [2000] 1 ILRM 193

> '... would, of course, be significantly eroded if at the subsequent trial of the person concerned the jury could be invited to draw inferences adverse to him from his failure to reply to those questions and, specifically, to his failure to give the questioning Gardaí an account similar to that subsequently given by him in evidence. It would also render virtually meaningless the caution required to be given to him under the Judges' rules'.

Adverse inferences could not be drawn from silence in the absence of 'any express statutory provisions entitling a Court or jury to draw inferences from such silence'.

Therefore, adverse inferences can only be drawn from silence when permitted under legislation.

- *People (DPP) v Coddington*[439]

Murray J considered an accused's failure to give evidence at trial and concluded that:

> 'While the trial judge may remind the jury of the fact that the accused had, as it is right, not given evidence in the trial, they must be expressly instructed not to draw any inferences from the exercise of that right.'

- *Rock v Ireland*[440]

Hamilton CJ

> '... an inference could not form the basis for a conviction in the absence of other evidence and...only inferences as appeared proper to the Court could be drawn.'

- *Re National Irish Bank Limited*[441]

---

[439] 31 May 2001, unreported, Court of Criminal Appeal
[440] [1998] 2 ILRM 38
[441] [1990] ILRM 321

Barrington J:

> 'It is proper therefore to make clear that what is objectionable under Article 38 of the Constitution is compelling a person to confess and then convicting him on the basis of his compelled confession.'

- *Curtain v Clerk of Dail Eireann*[442]

Murray CJ:

> '... it is appropriate to draw attention to the distinction between a requirement that a person make a statement or give evidence which may tend to incriminate him and a requirement that a person produce for inspection whether by the Garda Síochána or other organs of the State a physical article, including a document.'

The right to silence/privilege against self incrimination does not apply in respect of the latter circumstances.

Right to Defend Oneself

Re Haughey[443],

As per O' Dalaigh CJ, an accused has a right to defend himself which right, includes:

> '(*a*) that he should be furnished with a copy of the evidence which reflected on his good name; (*b*) that he should be allowed to cross-examine, by counsel, his accuser or accusers; (*c*) that he should be allowed to give rebutting evidence; and (*d*) that he should be permitted to address, again by counsel, the Committee in his own defence.'

[442] [2006] IESC 27
[443] [1971] IR 217

Right of Access to a Solicitor

- *The People (DPP) v Healy*[444]

An accused has a right of reasonable access to a solicitor.

- *DPP v Finnegan*[445]

The access to a solicitor must be in private.

- *Lavery v The Member in Charge, Carrickmacross Garda Station*[446]

O' Flaherty J:

> 'The solicitor is not entitled to be present at the interviews. Neither was it open to the respondent, or his solicitor, to prescribe the manner by which the interviews might be conducted, or where.'

- *The People v Buck*[447]

The Gardaí are not prohibited from questioning a detainee pending the arrival of a solicitor:

- *O' Brien v DPP*[448]

Where the Gardaí purposefully deprive the detainee of access to a solicitor or delay in providing such access, any inculpatory statements made prior to the arrival of the solicitor are inadmissible.

In this case, McCracken J further held that:

---

444 [1990] 2 IR 73
445 15 July 1997, unreported, Court of Criminal Appeal
446 [1999] 2 IR 390
447 [2002] 2 IR 268
448 5 May 2005, unreported, Supreme Court

> '...once the solicitor did attend and was consulted by the appellant, any unlawfulness in his detention would cease...I am satisfied that he was in lawful detention at the time he made the statements subsequent to the arrival of his solicitor and those statements were rightly admitted in evidence.'

Pre-Trial Publicity

Pre-trial publicity can be prejudicial to the accused's right to a fair trial and can influence the jury's verdict.

D v DPP[449]

Denham J:

> '...the applicant's right to fair procedures is superior to the community's right to prosecute. If there was a real risk that the accused would not receive a fair trial [due to pre-trial publicity] then there would be no question of the accused's right to a fair trial being balanced detrimentally against the community's right to have alleged crimes prosecuted.'

Z v DPP[450]

Finlay CJ cited with approval the decision in *D v DPP* and added that:

> '... where one speaks of an onus to establish a real risk of an unfair trial it necessarily and inevitably means an unfair trial which cannot be avoided by appropriate rulings and directions on the part of the trial judge. The risk is a real one but the unfairness of trial must be an unavoidable unfairness of trial.'

---

449 [1994] 2 IR 465

450 [1994] 2 IR 476

The risk of an unfair trial can be minimised by a direction to the jury and Finlay CJ held that:

> 'I take the view that a trial judge will be able in a specific way, and with considerable specific detail, to point out to a jury at the very commencement of the trial...that the controversy, media publicity, newspaper and magazine commentary...are wholly irrelevant to the trial and must be completely put out of their minds.'

In determining whether the accused's right to a fair trial has been undermined by pre-trial publicity the Court will consider the 'fade factor' namely that, due to the passage of time, the impact of publicity will have reduced.

In *Rattigan v DPP*[451] Carroll J made reference to the fade factor as follows:

> 'As far as adverse pre-trial publicity is concerned, the so-called fade factor is most important. If a reasonable time has elapsed between the publicity and the trial the risk is altogether smaller and this will be especially so if a trial is in a city such as Dublin and not in a small town where a crime has been committed.'

Right to a Speedy Trial

Article 38.1 includes a right to an early trial.

State (O' Connell) v Fawcitt[452]

Finlay CJ:

> '... a person charged with a criminal offence is entitled, as part of his right to be tried in due course of law, to a trial with reasonable expedition.'

[451] 7 May 2008, unreported, Supreme Court

[452] [1986] ILRM 639

Finlay CJ concluded that:

> '... if a person's trial has been excessively delayed so as to prejudice his chance of obtaining a fair trial, then the appropriate remedy by which the Constitutional rights of such an individual can be defended and protected is by an order of prohibition.'

The Supreme Court in *McFarlane v DPP*[453] adopted the decision of the United States Supreme Court in *Barker v Wingo*[454] wherein Powell J held that:

> '... prejudice [caused] by delay should be assessed in the light of the interests of defendants which the speedy trial right was designed to protect. This court has identified three such interests:
>
> (i) to prevent oppressive pre trial incarceration;
>
> (ii) to minimise anxiety and concern of the accused; and
>
> (iii) to limit the possibility that the defence will be impaired'

Powell J identified four factors to be considered when assessing delay:

- The length of the delay.
- The reasons given by the prosecution to justify the delay.
- The responsibility of the accused for asserting his rights and
- The prejudice to the accused.

---

453 5 March 2008, unreported, Supreme Court

454 407 US 514 (1972)

In *B v DPP*[455] Denham J held that the following factors should be considered in assessing cases of delay:

'(i) The delay in the case;

(ii) The reason or reasons for delay;

(iii) The accused's actions in relation to the events in issue;

(iv) The accused's assertion of his constitutional rights;

(v) Actual prejudice to the accused;

(vi) Pre-trial incarceration of the accused;

(vii) Length of time of pre-trial anxiety and concern of the accused;

(viii) Limitations or impairment of defence;

(ix) Circumstances which may render the case into a special category;

(x) The community's right to have offences prosecuted.'

P.M. v Malone[456]

Keane CJ:

> 'Where there has been significant and culpable delay to which [the accused] has not contributed in any way, the result may be either actual prejudice (the loss of otherwise available evidence) or presumptive prejudice (the difficulties necessarily inherent in giving evidence after a lengthy period) which may affect his ability to defend himself and hence fatally compromise the fairness of the trial.'

---

455 [1997] 3 IR 140

456 [2002] 2 IR 560

The Supreme Court in *P.M. v DPP*[457] endorsed the decision of Keane CJ in *P.M. v Malone*[458] that:

> 'Where, as here, the violation of the right has not jeopardised the right to a fair trial, but has caused unnecessary stress and anxiety to the applicant, the Court must engage in a balancing process. On one side of the scales, there is the right of the accused to be protected from stress and anxiety caused by an unnecessary and inordinate delay. On the other side, there is the public interest in the prosecution and conviction of those guilty of criminal offences. In all such cases, the Court will necessarily be concerned with the nature of the offence and the extent of the delay.'

The test to be applied in cases of child abuse where the victim has delayed in coming forward was set out by Denham J in the Supreme Court in *B v DPP*[459]:

> 'The test is therefore whether there is a real risk that the accused by reason of the delay would not obtain a fair trial. The test must be applied in light in the light of the case and the law.'

In *H v DPP*[460] Murray CJ stated that in considering issues of delay in child abuse cases the Court should have regard to factors such as 'dominion, inhibition, disparity between the ages of the accused and the complaint' and in *P.O'C v DPP*[461] Murray J further advised that case law has demonstrated that:

---

457 [2006] 3 IR 172
458 [2002] 2 IR 560
459 [1997] 3 IR 140
460 31 July 2006, unreported, Supreme Court
461 [2000] 3 IR 87

'...young or very young victims of sexual abuse are often very reluctant or find it impossible to come forward and disclose the abuse to others or in particular to complain to Gardaí until many years later (if at all). In fact this has been so clearly demonstrated in a succession of cases that the Court would probably be entitled to take judicial notice of the fact that this is an inherent element in the nature of such offences.'

Preservation of Evidence

Failure to seek out or preserve vital evidence is a breach of the right to a fair trial.

In *Braddish v DPP*[462] the Supreme Court endorsed the decision of the High Court in *Murphy v DPP*[463] on the duty to preserve evidence wherein Lynch J stated that "the authorities established that evidence relevant to guilt or innocence must so far as is necessary and practicable be kept until the conclusion of the trial. These authorities also apply to the preservation of articles which may give rise to the reasonable possibility of securing relevant evidence."

Hardiman J in Braddish stated that:

'It is the duty of the Gardaí, arising from their unique investigative role, to seek out and preserve all evidence having a bearing or potential bearing on the issue of guilt or innocence.'

However Hardiman J further opined that this duty

'...cannot be interpreted as requiring the Gardaí to engage in disproportionate commitment of manpower or

[462] [2001] 3 IR 127
[463] [1989] ILRM 71

> resources in an exhaustive search for every conceivable kind of evidence. The duty must be interpreted realistically on the facts of each case.'

In *Dunne v DPP*[464] Hardiman J held that the duty of the Gardaí "extends also to taking reasonable steps to seek out material evidence."

In *Bowes & McGrath v DPP*[465] Hardiman J cited with approval the decision of Lynch J in *Murphy v DPP*[466] that there will be a real risk of an unfair trial where an accused is deprived of the opportunity to carry out an inspection or examination of evidence where such inspection or examination would have offered "the reasonable possibility of rebutting the evidence proffered against him."

In *McFarlane v DPP*[467] Hardiman J ruled that failure to preserve primary evidence will not result in an unfair trial where such evidence is available in "an independent verifiable form."

Unconstitutionally Obtained Evidence

The exclusionary rule on the admissibility of unconstitutionally obtained evidence was first enunciated by Walsh J in the *People (AG) v O' Brien*[468]:

> 'In my view evidence obtained in deliberate and conscious breach of the constitutional rights of an accused person should, save in [extraordinary excusing circumstances], be absolutely inadmissible. It follows therefore that evidence

464 [2002] 2 ILRM 305
465 [2003] IESC 9
466 [1989] ILRM 71
467 7 March 2006, unreported, Supreme Court
468 [1965] IR 142

> obtained without a deliberate and conscious violation of the accused's Constitutional rights is not excluded by reason only of the violation of his constitutional rights.'

Instances of 'extraordinary excusing circumstances', per Walsh J, include:

> '... the need to prevent an imminent destruction of vital evidence or rescue of a person in peril, and the seizure of evidence obtained in the course of and incidental to a lawful arrest even though the premises on which the arrest is made have been entered without a search warrant.'

However in the *People (DPP) v Kenny*[469] the Supreme Court laid down an absolute exclusionary rule on unconstitutionally obtained evidence. Finlay CJ:

> '...evidence obtained by the invasion of the Constitutional personal rights of a citizen must be excluded unless a court is satisfied that either the act constituting the breach of Constitutional rights was committed unintentionally or accidentally, or is satisfied that there are extraordinary excusing circumstances which justify the admission of evidence in its discretion'.

It is immaterial whether a Garda was or was not aware that his actions were in breach of the Constitutional rights of the accused. Instead the test is whether the actions of the Garda, which resulted in the breach, was a conscious and deliberate act.

Finlay CJ outlined the objective of this approach as follows:

> 'To exclude only evidence obtained by a person who knows or ought reasonably to know that he is invading

[469] [1990] 2 IR 210

a Constitutional right is to impose a negative deterrent. It is clearly effective to dissuade a policeman from acting in a manner which he knows is unconstitutional or from acting in a manner reckless as to whether his conduct is or is not unconstitutional. To apply, on the other hand, the absolute protection rule of exclusion whilst providing also that negative deterrent, incorporates as well a positive encouragement to those in authority over the crime prevention and detection services of the State to consider in detail the personal rights of the citizens as set out in the Constitution, and the effect of their powers of arrest, detention, search and questioning in relation to such rights.'

In *DPP (Walsh) v Cash*[470] Fennelly J in the Supreme Court ruled that the absolute exclusionary rule in Kenny related only to the exclusion of evidence proferred at trial and is does not concern "the lawful provenance of evidence used to ground a suspicion" for a lawful arrest.

Fennelly J held that:

'It has never been held that what would be found a reasonable suspicion in law, requires to be based on the kind of evidence that would be admissible under the rules of evidence during the hearing of a criminal trial. On the contrary, a reasonable suspicion can be based on hearsay evidence or can be inferred from discovering that an alibi which a suspect has given to the police turns out to be false.'

Illegally Obtained Evidence

In relation to evidence obtained in contravention of the law or legal rights, Kingsmill Moore J in *O' Brien* ruled

[470] [2010] IESC 1

that a trial judge has discretion whether to admit or exclude illegally obtained evidence through a consideration of all the circumstances of the case and, in particular, the nature and extent of the illegality:

> 'Was the illegal action intentional or unintentional, and, if intentional, was it the result of an ad hoc decision or does it represent a settled and deliberate policy? Was the illegality one of a trivial and technical nature or was it a serious invasion of important rights the recurrence of which would involve a real danger to necessary freedoms? Were there circumstances of urgency or emergency which provide some excuse for the action?'

Other Aspects of Trial in Due Course of Law

- *King v AG*[471]

An accused can only be convicted of a criminal offence 'if the ingredients of, and the acts constituting the offence, are specified with precision and clarity.'

- *O' Callaghan v Ireland*[472]

In this case, Finlay CJ held that a member of An Garda Síochána must exercise powers of stop, search and arrest:

> '... in a Constitutional manner. If any member of the Garda Síochána should in the purported exercise of the powers conferred on him.... expose any person to unnecessary harassment, distress or embarrassment, it would be an abuse of the powers and an unconstitutional violation of that person's rights for which that person would have the appropriate and correct remedies'.

[471] [1981] IR 233
[472] [1994] 1 IR 554

Finlay CJ further advised that in determining whether the exercise of such powers is Constitutionally permissible the court will consider whether the interference with the personal rights of the accused is proportionate to the interest of the common good in combating the subject crime.

- An accused cannot be prosecuted in respect of an offence of which he was previously acquitted (*autrefois acquit*) or previously convicted (*autrefois convict*).

Registrar of Companies v Judge David Anderson & Anor[473]
Murray CJ:

> '...if a person is prosecuted for an offence arising out of the same breach of the law or the same essential ingredients for which he has previously been tried and either convicted or acquitted, his defence to the second prosecution will be based on the pleas of autrefois acquit or autrefois convict. If either plea is successful the prosecution may proceed no further.'

[473] [2004] IESC 103

21

Directive Principles of Social Policy

Article 45

Article 45 of the Constitution provides that:

> 'The principles of social policy set forth in this Article are intended for the general guidance of the Oireachtas. The application of those principles in the making of laws shall be the care of the Oireachtas exclusively, and shall not be cognisable by any Court under any of the provisions of this Constitution.'

The principles of social policy are listed thereafter to include, *inter alia,* the following:

- The State must strive to promote the welfare of the people and justice and charity must inform all the institutions of the national life.
- Citizens have a right to an adequate means of livelihood.
- The ownership and control of the material resources and the operation of free competition must be regulated in the interests of the common good and essential commodities must not be placed in the hands of a few.

- The State must favour and supplement, where necessary, private initiative in industry and commerce and the state must ensure reasonable efficiency in private industry in the production and distribution of goods and protect the public against unjust exploitation.
- The State must protect the weaker sections of the community, and, where necessary, contribute to the support of the infirm, the widow, the orphan, and the aged.
- Citizens must not be forced by economic necessity to enter occupations unsuited to their sex, age or strength.

Guidance Only

The Directive Principles of Social Policy are specified as 'for the general guidance of the Oireachtas' and are 'not be cognisable by any Court.'

- *Comyn v Attorney General*[474]

Kingsmill Moore J:

> '[Article 45] puts the State under certain duties, but they are not duties of imperfect obligation since they cannot be enforced or regarded by any court of law and are only directions for the guidance of the Oireachtas.'

- *O' Brien v Manufacturing Engineering Company Limited*[475]

[474] [1950] IR 142
[475] [1973] IR 334, (1974) 108 ILTR 105

Pringle J:

> '...the Courts cannot enquire into the question as to whether the Oireachtas has implemented [the provisions of Article 45]'.

Application of the Principles

- *Murtagh Properties v Cleary*[476]

Kenny J, in recognising that an unenumerated right to earn a livelihood was derived from Article 45, held that, while the Courts:

> 'have no jurisdiction to consider the application of the principles in [Article 45] in the making of laws', the Courts may take Article 45 'into consideration when deciding whether a claimed constitutional right exists.'

- *Landers v Attorney General*[477]

Finlay P. stated that he would have:

> 'some regard to the directive principles of social policy laid down in Article 45 when considering the constitutionality of a pre-Constitution statute.'

- *Nova Media Services v Minister for Posts and Telegraphs*[478] and *Attorney General v Paperlink*[479]

The provisions of Article 45 were cited as reflecting a Constitutional preference for private enterprise over State monopoly.

476 [1972] IR 330
477 (1973) 109 ILTR 1
478 [1984] ILRM 161
479 [1984] ILRM 373

- *Kerry Co-Operative Creameries Ltd v An Bord Bainne*[480]

McCarthy J held that the doctrine of restraint of trade should be considered having regard to the provisions of Article 45 and that:

> 'the exclusion of the application of the Article by any Court in respect of the making of laws, does not exclude their consideration in the construction of the common law.'

- *McGee v Attorney General*[481]

O' Keeffe P in the High Court espoused that Article 45 appears

> 'to exclude from the cognisance of the Courts only questions as to the attempts of the Oireachtas to have regard to the principles laid down in the course of framing legislation, and it may be argued that it does not preclude the consideration of these principles by the Courts when a statute of the Oireachtas is not under review'.

Fitzgerald CJ in the Supreme Court affirmed that:

> 'Article 45 refers to principles of social policy which are intended for the general guidance of the Oireachtas in its making of laws and which are declared to be exclusively its province and not cognisable by any Court. In my opinion, the intervention by this, or any other Court, with the function of the Oireachtas is expressly prohibited under this Article. To hold otherwise would be an invalid usurpation of legislative authority.'

---

480 [1991] ILRM 851
481 [1974] IR 284, (1975) 109 ILTR 29

22

Constitutionality of Legislation

Article 34.3.2 provides that:

> 'Save as otherwise provided by this Article, the jurisdiction of the High Court shall extend to the validity of any law having regard to the provisions of this Constitution and no such questions shall be raised by any Court established under this or any other Article of this Constitution other than the High Court or the Supreme Court.'

Jurisdiction

The Constitutionality of post 1937 legislation can only be assessed by the superior courts (High Court and Supreme Court). The lower courts (District Court, Circuit Court, Court of Criminal Appeal and Special Criminal Courts) are prohibited from considering the Constitutionality of post 1937 legislation.

In addition, the lower courts cannot state a case to the superior courts to consider the Constitutionality of legislation: *Foyle Fisheries Commission v Gallen*[482], *Minister for Labour v Costello*[483], *The People (DPP) v Dougan*[484].

It would also appear from the decision of Keane CJ in *The People (DPP) v MS*[485] that no issue as to the Constitutionality of pre-1937 legislation can be raised in the lower courts.

- *Coughlan v Patwell*[486]

The lower courts can enforce express Constitutional rights and those which have already been recognised in the Superior Courts.

- *IOT v B*[487]

The lower courts do not have jurisdiction to identify a new Constitutional right.

Presumption of Constitutionality

There is a presumption of Constitutionality in respect of post 1937 legislation. There is no such presumption in respect of pre-1937 legislation.

The State (Sheerin) v Kennedy[488]

482 (1960) Ir Jur Rep 35
483 [1988] IR 235
484 [1996] 1 IR 544
485 [2003] 1 IR 606
486 [1993] 1 IR 31, [1992] ILRM 808
487 [1998] 2 IR 321
488 [1966] IR 379

Walsh J:

> 'All laws in force on the date immediately prior to the coming into operation of the Constitution are presumed not to be in conflict with the Constitution in force at the date of their enactment or in excess of the powers of the parliament which enacted them, but they enjoy no such presumption in respect of the provisions of the present Constitution and fall to be examined under the provisions of Article 50 of the Constitution - not as to their validity but, even assuming they were valid, as to whether or not they are inconsistent with the provisions of the present Constitution.'

The presumption of Constitutionality in respect of post 1937 legislation was enunciated by Hanna J in *Pigs Marketing Board v Donnelly*[489]:

> 'When the Court has to consider the Constitutionality of a law it must, in the first place, be accepted as an axiom that a law passed by the Oireachtas, the elected representatives of the people, is presumed to be Constitutional unless and until the contrary is clearly established.'

The Constitutionality of post 1937 legislation was affirmed by the Supreme Court in *Re Article 26* and the *Offences Against the State (Amendment) Bill 1940*[490].

However in *M v An Bord Uchtála*[491] it was held that the presumption does not apply to legislation which is clearly unconstitutional.

489 [1939] IR 413
490 [1940] IR 470, [1940] 74 ILTR 61
491 [1977] IR 287

Mootness

Goold v Collins[492]

Hardiman J:

> 'A proceeding may be said to be moot where there is no longer any legal dispute between the parties... I believe that the present case is moot in the sense that it does not feature a live, concrete dispute between the parties: a decision on the outstanding issues [relating to the constitutionality of the relevant legislation] would have no direct impact on the parties.'

Under the principle of self-restraint/mootness the constitutionality of a statute will only be considered when necessary to determine the case before the Court.

In *The State (P Woods) v Attorney General*[493] Henchy J found that:

> '...a Court should not enter upon a question of Constitutionality unless it is necessary for the determination of the case before it.'

Murphy v Roche[494]

Finlay CJ:

> '...where the issues between the parties can be determined and finally disposed of by the resolution of an issue of law other than Constitutional law, the Court should proceed to determine that issue first and, if it determines the case, should refrain from expressing any view on the constitutional issue that may have been raised.'

492 [2004] IEHC 38
493 [1969] IR 385
494 [1987] IR 106

McDaid v Sheehy[495]

Finlay CJ:

> '...the Courts should not engage in the question of the possible invalidity of an Act of the Oireachtas unless it is necessary for its decision to do so'

White v Dublin City Council Ireland and The Attorney General[496]

Fennelly J:

> '...it is well-established in the case law of this Court that a challenge to the Constitutionality of a statute will not normally be addressed until the person mounting the challenge shows that he is affected by the provision.'

However Finlay CJ in *Murphy v Roche*[497] concluded that such a determination was subject 'to the overriding consideration of doing justice between the parties.'

Additionally in *M v An Bord Uchtála*[498], O' Higgins CJ held that:

> '[T]here may be circumstances of an exceptional nature where the requirements of justice and the protection of constitutional rights make the larger enquiry necessary.'

Double Construction Rule

The double construction rule was outlined by Walsh J in *McDonald v Bord Na gCon*[499]:

495 [1991] 1 IR 1, [1991] ILRM 250
496 [2004] 1 IR 545
497 [1987] IR 106
498 [1977] IR 287
499 [1965] IR 217

> '[I]n respect of any provision or provisions of the Act where two or more Constructions are reasonably open one of which is Constitutional and the other or others are unconstitutional it must be presumed that the Oireachtas intended only the Constitutional construction...'

East Donegal Co-Operative Limited v Attorney General[500]
Walsh J:

> 'An Act of the Oireachtas, or any provision thereof, will not be declared to be invalid where it is possible to construe it in accordance with the Constitution; and it is not only a question of preferring a constitutional construction to one which would be unconstitutional where they both may appear to be open, but it also means than an interpretation favouring the validity of an Act should be given in cases of doubt'

However Walsh J further held that:

> 'It must be added, of course, that interpretation or construction of an Act or any provision thereof in conformity with the Constitution cannot be pushed to the point where the interpetation would result in the substitution of the legislative provision by another provision with a different context, as that would be to usurp the functions of the Oireachtas. In seeking to reach an interpretation or construction in accordance with the Constitution, a statutory provision which is clear and unambiguous cannot be given an opposite meaning.'

Note also: *Attorney General v Conmey*[501]

---

500 [1970] IR 317, (1970) 104 ILTR 81
501 [1975] IR 341

Locus Standi

A party can only challenge the Constitutionality of legislation where he/she has *locus standi.*

Cahill v Sutton[502]

Henchy J:

> 'The primary rule as to standing in constitutional matters is that the person challenging the Constitutionality of the statute ... must be able to assert that, because of the alleged unconstitutionality, his [interests] have been adversely affected, or stand in real or imminent danger of being adversely affected by the statute ... [T]he stated rule of personal standing may be waived or relaxed if, in the particular circumstances of the case, the Court finds that there are weighty countervailing circumstances justifying a departure from the rule.'

Henchy J further espoused that:-

> 'This rule, however, being but a rule of practice must, like all such rules, be subject to expansion, exception or qualification when the justice of the case so requires'

Exceptions to the *locus standi* rule in *Cahill v Sutton*:

- Prejudiced party is unable to assert rights

In *SPUC v Coogan*[503] Finlay CJ acknowledged that, having regard to the circumstances of the particular case, there could never be a 'victim or potential victim who could sue.'

- Actio Popularis

502 [1980] IR 269
503 [1989] IR 734, [1990] ILRM 70

This arises where the subject matter of the proceedings affects the interests and rights of the public as a whole.

Crotty v An Taoiseach[504]
Finlay CJ:

> '...where the impugned legislation, namely the [Single European Act], will, if made operative, affect every citizen, the plaintiff has a *locus standi* to challenge the Act notwithstanding his failure to prove the threat of any special injury or prejudice to him, as distinct from any other citizen, arising from the Act.'

- Bona Fide Plaintiff

This occurs where the plaintiff has a genuine and *bona fide* interest in the subject matter of the proceedings.

In *SPUC v Coogan*[505] Finlay CJ determined that a party has sufficient *locus standi* where he/she has 'a *bona fide* interest and concern' in the subject of the proceedings and Walsh J held that "every member of the public has an interest in seeing that the fundamental law of the State is not defeated."

Jus Terti Rule

The Courts will only listen to arguments based on the plaintiff's own personal situation and will not allow arguments based on the circumstances of a third party.

Cahill v Sutton[506]

504 [1987] IR 713, [1987] ILRM 400
505 [1989] IR 734, [1990] ILRM 70
506 [1980] IR 269

Henchy J:

'The plaintiff is seeking to be allowed to conjure up, invoke and champion the putative Constitutional rights of a hypothetical third party... [the jus tertii rule] means that the challenger must adduce circumstances showing that the impugned provision is operating, or is poised to operate, in such a way as to deprive him personally of the benefit of a particular constitutional right.'

Madigan v Attorney General[507]

O'Hanlon J:

'The plaintiffs must be confined to argue the unconstitutionality of the statutory provisions challenged, insofar as they themselves are prejudiced thereby, and not by reference to other hypothetical cases which may arise for consideration under the Act.'

Note also: *Norris v Attorney General*[508], *King v Attorney General*[509], *A v Governor of Arbour Hill Prison*[510], *Riordan v Government of Ireland*[511].

Consequences of a Declaration of Unconstitutionality

Article 15.4.2

'Every law enacted by the Oireachtas which is in any respect repugnant to this Constitution or to any provision thereof, shall, but to the extent only of such repugnancy, be invalid.'

507 [1986[ILRM 136
508 [1984] IR 36
509 [1981] IR 233
510 31 July 2006, unreported, Supreme Court
511 [2009] IESC 44

Article 50.1 provides that pre-1937 legislation remains operative except to the extent that it is inconsistent with the Constitution.

Severance

A severability test was developed by the Supreme Court in *Maher v Attorney General*[512].

> 'The application of the doctrine of severability or separability in the judicial review of legislation has the effect that if a particular provision is held to be unconstitutional, and that provision is independent of and severable from the rest, only the offending provision will be declared invalid. The question is one of interpretation of the legislative intent.... But if what remains is so inextricably bound up with the part held invalid that the remainder cannot survive independently, or if the remainder would not represent the legislative intent, the remaining part will not be severed and given constitutional validity.'

Void ab initio

- *McDonnell v Ireland*[513]

Where a declaration of unconstitutionality is made in respect of post 1937 legislation the act or provision will be void *ab initio*.

- *Murphy v Attorney General*[514]

512 [1973] IR 140
513 [1998] 1 IR 134
514 [1982] IR 241

Where a declaration of unconstitutionality is made in respect of pre 1937 legislation the act or provision will be void from 1937 onwards.

Henchy J held that a claim for redress can be made by an aggrieved party where an act or provision is declared unconstitutional:

> 'Once it has been judicially established that a statutory provision enacted by the Oireachtas is repugnant to the Constitution, and that it therefore incurred invalidity from the date of its enactment, the condemned provision will normally provide no legal justification for any acts done or left undone, or for transactions undertaken in pursuance of it; and the person damnified by the operation of the invalid provision will normally be accorded by the Courts all permitted and necessary redress.'

The primary rule of redress however is subject to exceptions, particularly based on public policy grounds and in order to avoid injustice. Henchy J stated that:

> 'Over the centuries the law has come to recognise, in one degree or another that factors such as prescription (negative or positive), waiver, estoppel, laches, a statute of limitation, *res judicata*, or other matters (most of which may be grouped under the heading of public policy) may debar a person from obtaining redress... For a variety of reasons, the law recognises that in certain circumstances, no matter how unfounded in law certain conduct may have been, no matter how unwarranted its operation in a particular case, what has happened has happened and cannot, or should not, be undone. The irreversible progressions and byeproducts of time, the compulsion of public order and of the common good, the aversion of the law from giving a hearing to those who have slept on their rights, the quality

of legality - even irreversibility - that tends to attach to what has become inveterate or has been widely accepted or acted upon, the recognition that even in the short term the accomplished fact may sometimes acquire an inviolable sacredness, these and other factors may convert what has been done under an unconstitutional, or otherwise void, law into an acceptable part of the corpus juris.'

A v Governor of Arbour Hill Prison[515]

Murray J:

'...the retrospective effect of a judicial decision [on the Constitutionality of legislation] is excluded from cases already finally determined.'

Note also: *McMahon v Attorney General*[516], *De Burca v Attorney General*[517], *State (Byrne) v Frawley*[518], *McDonnell v Ireland*[519].

Emergency Legislation

Article 28.3.3 enables the Oireachtas enact emergency legislation in times of war or armed rebellion or in the aftermath of any such conflict, whether or not the State is a participant in any such conflict, for the purpose of securing the public safety and the preservation of the State.

Each House of the Oireachtas must have resolved that, arising out of the armed conflict, a national emergency exists which affects the vital interests of the State. Any

515 31 July 2006, unreported, Supreme Court
516 [1972] IR 69, (1972) 106 ILTR 89
517 [1976] IR 38, (1977) 111 ILTR 37
518 [1978] IR 326
519 [1998] 1 IR 134

such emergency legislation is immune from challenge as to its constitutionality.

In *Re McGrath and Harte*[520] the Supreme Court considered a challenge to the Emergency Powers (Amendment) (No. 2) Act 1940 and determined that:

> '...the clear language of [Article 28.3.3], which, in the times and circumstances contemplated, makes it impossible to invoke other Articles of the Constitution to invalidate Acts by the Oireachtas and expressed to be for the purpose of securing the public safety and the preservation of the State within the terms of the Article.'

In *The State (Walsh) v Lennon*[521] Gavan Duffy J, assessing a further challenge to the Emergency Powers (Amendment) (No. 2) Act 1940, espoused that:

> '...in time of war or armed conflict...the Constitution has placed in the hands of the Oireachtas, as law-giver, special authority to suspend judicial control over other organs of government during any such emergency... The plain intention [of Article 28.3.3] is that the natural guardian of the citizen's guarantees, the High Court of Justice in this State, shall for the time being relinquish its guardianship...'

In *Re Article 26 and the Emergency Powers Bill 1976*[522] the Supreme Court held that a Bill derived from Article 28.3.3 could be subject to an Article 26 however

> '... if it is shown to the Court that the preliminary and procedural requirements for the passing of the bill by both Houses of the Oireachtas have been complied with,

520 [1941] IR 68
521 [1942] IR 112
522 [1977] IR 159

it is *ipso facto*, because of the exemption granted by Article 28, s 3, ss 3, incapable of being struck down on the ground of repugnancy to the Constitution or to any provision thereof.'

However O' Higgins CJ cautioned that any act done arising from such legislation must be in strict conformity with its express provisions and that a party

'...may also rely on provisions of the Constitution for the purpose of construing [the Act] and of testing the legality of what has been done in purported operation of it.'

23

Constitution and International Law

A monist state is one in which international law automatically becomes part of the domestic legal system. A dualist state is one in which international law does not automatically become part of the domestic legal system.

Ireland is a dualist state by virtue of Article 29.6 of the Constitution which provides that:

> 'No international agreement shall be part of the domestic law of the state save as may be determined by the Oireachtas.'

Therefore the provisions of international law cannot be enforced against the State until such time as the State has incorporated such provisions into Irish law by legislation.

Kavanagh v Governor of Mountjoy Prison[523]

Fennelly J:

> 'The Constitution establishes an unmistakable distinction between domestic and international law...Where the government wishes the terms of an international agreement to have effect in domestic law, it may ask the

[523] [2002] 3 IR 97, [2002] 2 ILRM 81

Oireachtas to pass the necessary legislation. If this does not happen, article 29, section 6 applies.'

International Customary Law

International customary law is unenforceable against the state unless it has been incorporated by the legislature.

Horgan v Ireland[524]

Kearns J:

> '...international law is only admissible in domestic law to the extent already indicated where in certain limited situations it may be availed of to determine private law claims, absent some contrary or conflicting provision of either the Constitution, statute law or common law. It may also avail other States in their dealings with this State on the international plane. It cannot however impose binding public law obligations on the Executive towards its own citizens under Article 29 for all the reasons stated.'

European Union Law

A fundamental principle of the law of the European Union is that EU law prevails over the domestic law of the member states.

The supremacy of EU law was first established by the Court of Justice in *Van Gend en Loos*[525]:

> '...the Community constitutes a new legal order of international law for the benefit of which the states have limited their sovereign rights, albeit in limited fields...'

---

[524] [2003] 2 IR 468

[525] Case 26/62 *NV Algemene Transporten Expeditie Onderneming van Gen en Loos v Nederlandse Administratie der Belastingen* [1963] ECR 1

In the case of conflict between community law and national law, community law is to prevail.

Costa V Enel[526]:

> '[T]he transfer by the states from their domestic legal system to the Community legal system of the rights and obligations arising under the treaty carries with it a permanent limitation of their sovereign rights, against which a subsequent unilateral law incompatible with the aims of the Community cannot prevail.'

The supremacy of EU law over national law is enshrined in Article 29.4.10 of Bunreacht na hÉireann which states that:

> 'No provision of this Constitution invalidates laws enacted, acts done or measures adopted by the State which are necessitated by the obligations of membership of the European Union or of the Communities, or prevents laws enacted, acts done or measures adopted by the European Union or by the Communities or by institutions thereof, or by bodies competent under the Treaties establishing the Communities, from having the force of law in the State.'

In addition Article 2 of the European Communities Act 1972 states that:

> ... the treaties governing the European Communities and the existing and future acts adopted by the institutions of those Communities shall be binding on the State and shall be part of the domestic law thereof under the conditions laid down in those treaties.'

[526] Case 6/64 *Flaminio Costa v ENEL* [1964] ECR 585

Crotty v An Taoiseach[527]

Barrington J referred to Article 29.4.10 as "a very far-reaching amendment to the provisions of the Constitution" the implications of which are that:

> '... the Constitution could not now be invoked to invalidate any measure which the State was directed by the institutions of the EEC to take arising out of the exercise of their powers nor to invalidate any regulation or any decision of the European Court which had direct effect within this State by virtue of the provisions of the Treaties.'

Finlay CJ also referred to Article 29.4.3 which permitted Ireland to join the European Coal and Steel Community, the European Atomic Energy Community and the European Economic Community and held that this Article:

> '... must be construed as an authorisation given to the State not only to join the Communities as they stood in 1973, but also to join in amendments of the Treaties so long as such amendments do not alter the essential scope or objective of the Communities.'

Accordingly any Treaty which alters 'the essential scope or objective of the Communities' requires a constitutional amendment.

European Convention on Human Rights

Prior to the incorporation of the European Convention on Human Rights into Irish Law with the enactment of the European Convention on Human Rights Act 2003 it was not possible to rely on the provisions of the Convention in an Irish Court.

527 [1987] IR 713, [1987] ILRM 400

Re O' Laighleis[528]

Maguire CJ:

> '... the Oireachtas has not determined that the Convention...is to be part of the domestic law of the State and, accordingly this Court cannot give effect to the Convention if it be contrary to domestic law or purports to grant rights or impose obligations additional to those of domestic law.'

The salient provisions of the 2003 Act are as follows:

- Section 2: The Courts are to interpret and apply law in a manner compatible with the Convention.
- Section 3: Every organ of the State must perform its functions in a manner compatible with the States obligations under the Convention provisions and a person may recover damages where he/she who has suffered injury, loss or damage as a result of a contravention.
- Section 4: The Courts must take account of the judgments of the European Court of Human Rights when interpreting and applying the Convention.
- Section 5: The High Court can make a declaration of incompatibility where a statutory provision or rule of law is incompatible with the State's obligations under the Convention however any such declaration will not affect the validity, continuing operation or enforcement of the statutory provision or rule of law.

Dublin City Council v Fennell[529]

---

528 [1960] IR 93, (1961) 95 ILTR 92

529 [2005] IESC 33

Kearns J held that the convention was:

'... incorporated in Ireland at a sub-constitutional level in a form of indirect or interpretative incorporation adopted by the 2003 Act.'

24

Amending the Constitution

Article 46 of the Constitution provides that:

'1. Any provision of this Constitution may be amended, whether by way of variation, addition, or repeal, in the manner provided by this Article.

2. Every proposal for an amendment of this Constitution shall be initiated in Dáil Éireann as a Bill, and shall upon having been passed or deemed to have been passed by both Houses of the Oireachtas, be submitted by Referendum to the decision of the people in accordance with the law for the time being in force relating to the Referendum.'

The Constitution can only be amended by referendum put to the people.

Judicial Interference with Referendum

There can be no judicial Interference to prevent a referendum or challenge its outcome.

Roche v Ireland[530]

Carroll J

'A constitutional amendment is a particularly solemn legislative process; not only the Oireachtas but also the people took part. With this process the Courts have no jurisdiction to interfere.'

The Courts do not have jurisdiction to assess the constitutionality of a Bill which is to be voted upon by the people.

Finn v Minister for the Environment[531]

O' Higgins CJ:

> 'The judicial power to review legislation on the ground of Constitutionality is confined (save in cases to which Article 26 of the Constitution applies) to enacted laws. Save in these excepted cases, there is no jurisdiction to construe or to review the Constitutionality of a Bill, whatever its nature. The Courts have no power to interfere with the legislative process'.

Furthermore, the Courts will not grant an injunction to prevent an injunction being put to the people.

Slattery v An Taoiseach[532]

McCarthy J:

> 'The plaintiff sought the intervention of the Courts, the judicial organ of Government, to arrest this Constitutional procedure, involving both the legislative and executive organs of government, and, further, involving the source

---

530 17 June 1983, unreported, High Court

531 [1983] IR 154

532 [1993] 1 IR 286

of all powers of Government, the People...to grant an Order such as sought would be a wholly unwarranted and unwarrantable intervention by the judiciary in what is clearly a legislative and popular domain.'

The Courts are therefore reluctant to intervene in the referendum process.

Note also: *Riordan v An Taoiseach (No. 1)*[533], *Riordan v An Taoiseach (No. 2)*[534], *Morris v Minister for Environment*[535], *Riordan v Government of Ireland*[536].

Similarly the courts will not challenge the outcome of a referendum.

Hanafin v Minister for Environment[537]

Hamilton CJ:

'The will of the people as expressed in a referendum providing for the amendment of the Constitution is sacrosanct and if freely given, cannot be interfered with. The decision is theirs and theirs alone.'

Riordan v An Taoiseach (No. 1)[538]

Barrington J:

'There can be no question of a constitutional amendment properly placed before the people and approved by them being itself unconstitutional.'

---

533 [1999] 4 IR 321

534 [1999] 4 IR 343

535 [2002] 1 IR 326

536 14 February 2002, unreported, High Court; 4 March 2002, unreported, Supreme Court

537 [1996] 2 IR 321

538 [1999] 4 IR 321

Note also: *Re Article 26* and the *Information (Termination of Pregnancies) Bill 1995*[539].

Funding of Referendum Campaigns

McKenna Principles

McKenna v An Taoiseach (No. 2)[540]

Hamilton CJ:

> 'The Courts have no power, either express or implied, to supervise or interfere with the exercise by the Government of its executive functions provided that it acts within the restraints imposed by the Constitution on the exercise of such powers, [however], if the Government acts otherwise than in accordance with the provisions of the Constitution and in clear disregard thereof, the Courts are not only entitled but obliged to intervene.'
>
> 'The use by the Government of public funds to fund a campaign designed to influence the voters in favour of a 'Yes' vote is an interference with the democratic process and the Constitutional process for the amendment of the Constitution and infringes the concept of equality which is fundamental to the democratic nature of the State'.

McCrystal v Minister for Children & Ors[541]

Denham CJ:

> '[T]he McKenna principles require that a publicly funded publication about a referendum must be fair, equal, impartial and neutral.'

Note also: *Coughlan v Broadcasting Complaints Committee*[542].

---

539 [1995] 1 IR 1, [1995] 2 ILRM 81

540 [1995] 2 IR 10, [1996] 1 ILRM 81

541 [2012] IESC 53

542 [2000] 3 IR 1

Index